THE REAL ESTATE PROFITING FROM THE REVOLUTION

Gail G. Lyons
Donald L. Harlan
John Tuccillo
Special Contributing Author

Real Estate
Education Company
a division of Dearborn Financial Publishing, Inc.

Acquisitions Editor: Christine E. Litavsky
Managing Editor: Jack Kiburz
Interior Design: Lucy Jenkins
Cover Design: David Corona Design

Published by Real Estate Education Company®,
a division of Dearborn Financial Publishing, Inc.®

Printed in the United States of America

97 98 10 9 8 7 6 5 4 3 2

Library of Congress Cataloging-in-Publication Data

Lyons, Gail G.
    The future of real estate : profiting from the revolution / by Gail Lyons, Don Harlan, John Tuccillo.
        p.   cm.
    Includes bibliographical references and index.
    ISBN 0-7931-1584-1 (pbk.)
    1. Real estate business—United States—Forecasting.   2. Economic forecasting—United States.   3. United States—Economic conditions—1993-.
4. Strategic planning—United States.
I. Harlan, Donald L.   II. Tuccillo, John A.   III. Title.
HD255.L95   1996
333.33—dc20
                                                                95-49433
                                                                CIP

Real Estate Education Company books are available at special quantity discounts to use as premiums and sales promotions, or for use in corporate training programs. For more information, please call the Special Sales Manager at 800-621-9621, ext. 4384, or write to Dearborn Financial Publishing, Inc., 155 N. Wacker Drive, Chicago, IL 60606-1719.

CONTENTS

PREFACE

We invite you to join us in this exploration of the future of real estate. Although some might question how we can explore territory that does not yet exist, it is our contention that *the future is here today* if only we will open our eyes and see it. Lao Tsu, a sixth century B.C. Chinese philosopher, perhaps said it best: "Knowing ignorance is strength, ignoring knowledge is sickness; how do I know the universe is like this? By looking!"

As you're aware, the universe around us is changing rapidly. It's our belief that the survivors in our industry, as in all others, will be those who can adapt and use these changes. Those who believe that business as usual will continue to support and protect them will not survive. Those who ride the waves of change will succeed and prosper. We suspect that the readers of this book are in the latter category. Congratulations!

Change seemingly characterizes every aspect of contemporary real estate practice. But because the mental models (paradigms) we use are themselves changing, the nature of change is fundamental, transformational and accelerating. These changes are occurring both in the larger world environment and, more specifically, within the real estate industry. The quantity and magnitude of these changes create turbulent, chaotic times in which success can be achieved only by those businesses and individuals that accurately *anticipate the future* by identifying critical changes and finding innovative solutions to the opportunities generated by them.

The goals and structure of *The Future of Real Estate: Profiting from the Revolution* are fourfold: (1) to analyze change and how to deal with it; (2) to identify the global and national changes that form the context within which the real estate industry must exist (many of these are either technological or demographic in character); (3) to describe the major changes or paradigm shifts occurring within the real estate industry itself and understand their character and potential effect on the businesses of individual real estate practitioners and the companies within which they work; and (4) to provide the key characteristics of effective strategies for creating a competitive edge in a world of change.

As authors, we presume to identify these changes and suggest methodologies for dealing with them because of our experiences and resultant observations over the past decades. Don and Gail have been successful real estate brokers since the early 1970s. Since 1986, they've also been leaders and change agents within the agency revolution, having taught in excess of 36,000 students throughout the United States as well as in Canada and Eastern Europe. They've also coauthored the leading textbooks in both buyer agency and dual agency and have simultaneously held numerous leadership roles at the local, state and national levels of organized real estate. Dr. John is well recognized nationally as the chief economist of the National Association of REALTORS®. As such, he predicts trends, not only in the economy but also in the ways in which business is done. His inimitable style makes both the complex and the obscure comprehensible.

PART ONE

Understanding Change and Its Effects

CHAPTER 1

Even Change Is Changing!

The very nature of change is changing. All dimensions of change are included: *Frequency, magnitude, complexity, rapidity* and *visibility* are all substantially increasing. The old adage that "the only thing that is constant is change" couldn't be more true.

Evolutionary change, the kind we've been used to, lets us move predictably into the future. Now change is accelerating so rapidly that the future explodes, changing before we have a chance to take advantage of the opportunities it offers. In other words, change that used to be sequential is now discontinuous and unpredictable. As a result, *we must change from planning for the future to preparing for the unexpected.* Strategic planning is no longer effective, because we literally don't have a clear enough vision of the future. The best we can do is short-term planning and strategic positioning.

Let's be more specific about these changes by looking historically at change. When we do, we see a series of overlapping waves, each of which is characterized by a unique technology. Linking these waves, we get the familiar historical pattern of the coexistence of old and new. For example, in 1910 it was usual to see horse-drawn wagons and horseless carriages on the same street. Change was relatively easy, because we could keep one foot in the old and one in the new. These waves of change are the single most important organizing principle of the late 20th/ early 21st century (see Figure 1.1).

Futurist Alvin Toffler, author of *Future Shock*, was the first to point out that Wave 1—agricultural technology—encompassed more than 100 generations and lasted approximately 6,000 years. Change happened slowly during this period, so people *knew* what the future would be like. Wave 2, the industrial era, arrived about 1760 and has lasted for nearly 300 years. Power began to pass from royalty, who gained title and land through inheritance, to those who "earned" it through better ideas— ideas that took advantage of mechanical technologies. This era is now rapidly coming to an end.

As significant as these change waves were, each was relatively flat and could be digested before the next wave overtook it. This is no longer true. Wave 3, the information age, began its upward trend in the mid-1960s and peaked about 1985, *in spite of the fact that most of us are just beginning to accomplish the reengineering necessary to adapt and transform our businesses.* The effective use of technology by business occurs long after the actual invention, it seems, resulting in an "impact gap." Compare the technologies listed in Figure 1.2 to the dates you first remember using them. Keep in mind that your purchase of a particular technology may have been triggered by a competitor using it first. That means companies today often are being "forced" to apply technology just to survive. The integration of these technologies into everyday practice and the effects they have will be explored in detail in Part II: Changing Trends in American Business.

FIGURE 1.1   Waves of Change

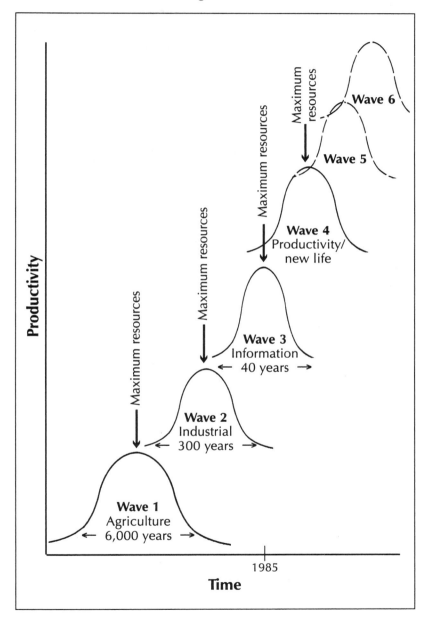

Although Wave 3 may not be complete for another ten years, Wave 4 is already upon us. Labeled the wave of productivity/ new life by Dudley Lynch and Paul Kordis, authors of *Strategy of the Dolphin*, it is driven mainly by bioengineering, robotics,

FIGURE 1.2   Information Technologies

Technology	Year Invented	Year I First Used/Knew About Technology
Television	1933	
Computer	early 1940s	
Transistor	1947	
Facsimile	1949	
Speech recognition by computers	1950	
Satellites	late 1950s	
Artificial heart	1963	
Computer mouse	1965	
Virtual reality	1965	
VCR	1970s	
Cellular telephone	1979	
Personal computer	1981	
Compact disc	1983	
Microchip	1984	
Cellular data link (modem)	1992	

new materials, machine cognition, nano-technology and exotic energy. We already know that some 800 body parts can be replaced bionically, and it has been shown that human neurons will grow on microchips, resulting in communication between human matter and machines.

During this fourth age, which has already begun, it's predicted that we'll actually experience what used to be solely the realm of science fiction: robots capable of doing much of what humans can do, including replication; the "curing" of genetic diseases that now account for over 60 percent of all patients in hospital beds; resurrection of extinct animals and plants as well as destroyed portions of rain forests and ocean floors; and human life extending to 150 or even 300 years, halting if not reversing the aging process. If even part of this is true, what will it mean for our daily lives and for the real estate industry in particular?

---

*S*tepping Ahead to Profit$

List the effects that some or all of the Wave 4 changes described above might have on your business.

Another model to explain the nature of the change is the *paradigm*. The ancient Greek word *paradeigma,* which means model, pattern or example, is the root of our definition. Until recently, the word was esoteric, heard only in academic conversations. Now it is heard frequently in the conversations of strategic planners and consultants in such diverse worlds as government, business/industry and education. Two of the leading business consultants/trainers/authors, Karl Albrecht (*The Only Thing That Matters*, 1992) and Joel A. Barker (*Paradigms: The*

Business of Discovering the Future, 1993) have further clarified the definition of paradigm. According to Albrecht, "A paradigm is a mental frame of reference that dominates the way people think and act." Barker adds, "A paradigm is a set of rules and regulations [written or unwritten] that does two things: (1) it establishes or defines boundaries, and (2) it tells you how to behave inside the boundaries in order to be successful."

Paradigm shifts may still seem esoteric until we look at some of the trends that have already become reality in real estate. Do you remember when all brokers split commissions fifty-fifty with their agents? No one questioned the split because everyone had always done it that way. But in 1971, a young man by the name of Dave Liniger, in one of Denver's Van Schaack & Company offices, questioned not only calculation of the split but the entire concept: "Why shouldn't agents receive 100 percent of the commission and pay their broker a monthly desk cost?" In the 24 years that have elapsed since Liniger asked his question, the answer, which is embodied in the RE/MAX franchise concept, has affected almost every real estate company: In order to compete effectively, almost all companies now offer at least a graduated commission split and many offer 100 percent.

Under the old fifty-fifty rule (or paradigm), broker-owners understood the game of how to run a successful real estate office. But the paradigm has shifted, there's a new set of rules in which agents hold the power and broker-owners struggle to improve a seemingly ever-shrinking bottom line.

Throughout the remaining chapters, we'll further explore the trends that mold our thinking and how to deal with them as they shift. Our business paradigms are based on past successes and failures. At the same time, they are strongly influenced by our collective culture—the values and habits of the individuals who make up both the real estate industry and the companies within it. As a result, paradigms can be both positive and negative. When we've just shifted into a new paradigm, it can be a real plus as we find new ways to solve problems, new ways to capitalize on opportunities. However, as our competitors also shift, the now "old" paradigm can become an invisible obstacle, a negative, as it has a tendency to blind us to other solutions and opportunities.

---

*S*tepping Ahead to Profit$

    Change is pervasive in today's real estate environment. Look at your own real estate business and write down specific, personal examples of some or all of the following generic changes:

- Redefinition of customer/client requirements
- Rapid development of new technologies
- Increased competition for goods and services
- Increased consumer expectations in value, quality and productivity
- Influence of government in business activity

Keep this list handy, adding to it and modifying it as you read future chapters. This will become a challenging outline for creating your own keys to future success, your competitive edge.

Future Thoughts

Change affects everything we do in terms of both our business and our personal lives. The model of historical waves of change clearly indicates that change itself is accelerating, making it increasingly difficult for real estate professionals to adapt to it, let alone take advantage of the opportunities it creates.

The paradigm model for change begins to give us clues as to how best to deal with change, knowing that paradigms are essentially a set of rules and regulations that can be identified. As we'll see in chapters to come, we can learn to detect changes in such rules and regulations and position ourselves on the leading edge of any significant paradigm change.

CHAPTER 2

Chaos: The Effect of Change

Because the very nature of change today is different, as well as the changes themselves, we tend to become disoriented. The changes are difficult to assimilate because we've lost our points of reference.

As an example of changes we're all familiar with that could cause disorientation (this model was first used by Jerry Matthews, EVP, Florida Association of REALTORS®), let me tell you about my family. My great-grandmother lived in a hand-made cabin in the mining camp of Nolan, just outside of Lyons, Colorado (just north of Boulder); she was born there in 1893. Try to imagine Moses (from the Bible) visiting my great-grandmother's home. He would probably find it very familiar: The house was built by my great-grandfather and some friends, the water came from a nearby spring, they hunted and raised all the food they ate, they occasionally used horses and wagons for transportation but mostly they walked. Perhaps the only thing that wouldn't look familiar was the shotgun hung over the mantle.

Now, let's imagine Moses visiting my home in the mountains just west of Boulder. Only three generations later, almost everything would seem very strange: There's a box with moving pictures, another box in which food cooks instantly and a strange metal vehicle with wheels that runs by burning a foul-smelling liquid; I talk on a hand-held instrument to people who live anywhere from next door to thousands of miles away, and sometimes I even fly to meet those people. My great-grandmother's life would seem familiar to Moses, while mine would seem strange and disorienting.

The Two Sides of Crisis

Change, especially the rapid, multidimensional change we're now experiencing in many aspects of our lives, often results in chaos. Chaos makes planning difficult if not impossible, for chaos is usually perceived as a series of crises. People describe crisis response variously as being "up to my waist in alligators" and as "fighting fires." Neither metaphor is very useful, as both conjure up images of threatening situations to which one would probably respond with fear.

A much more effective image of crisis can be obtained by looking at the Chinese word for *crisis* (see Figure 2.1). The Chinese calligraphy shows the two aspects of a concept; for *crisis*, these two sides of the same coin are *danger* and *opportunity*.

Many of us focus on danger and therefore become uncomfortable and fearful. Indeed, we often panic, resulting in a flurry of activity, "striking out at the alligators," while not knowing where or how we'll fit in or whether we have the skills to deal with the change. Our reaction often begins with *denial* that the change is actually occurring, followed by *anger* that this is happening, then *grief* that everything seems to be collapsing about us, and finally *acceptance* and a resolution to turn disadvantage into advantage. Change is nearly always both stressful and very time-consuming.

FIGURE 2.1　"Crisis" in Chinese

Those of us who concentrate on danger may have "paradigm paralysis," which causes us to see only the threats that come with change because we're boxed in by the rules and regulations of the current paradigm and can't see beyond it. New ideas are often "shot down" by people who have paradigm paralysis, who believe that the future is merely an extension of the past. Their current paradigm acts as a filter for incoming data, allowing them to select only those data that meet their expectations and fit their paradigm. They've often been the creators of the present and therefore have an emotional investment in preserving it.

Unfortunately, some with paradigm paralysis direct large, resource-rich companies with seemingly unrivaled track records and an attitude that "we can't fail." As a result, there's little or no sense of urgency, time-honored recipes for success are continually used and sometimes momentum is mistaken for leadership. As philosopher Eric Hoffer once remarked, "In times of change, learners inherit the earth, while the learned are simply beautifully equipped to lead a world that no longer exists."

Charting the Changes in Real Estate

Nancy Wilson-Smith, vice president and chief communication officer, National Association of REALTORS®, recently compiled two charts that illustrate the major shifts occurring within today's real estate industry (see Figure 2.2).

$\mathcal{S}$tepping Ahead to Profit$

Study these lists carefully; then highlight those words and phrases that describe your view of your current business world.

Often, as is certainly true with many of the changes in real estate, there is little evidence to prove that these changes are either occurring or have taken place. Unlike stable times, times of change require that many decisions be made. Often there is insufficient information on which to base decisions and intuitive judgment is required. As a result, "paradigm pioneers"—the ones who navigate the upriver currents of change—must have faith, trusting in their own judgment. Indeed, they must be courageous. To do this requires sufficient motivation to leave the familiar and move into a new unknown.

Such pioneers have the flexibility to see the opportunities offered by change and the advantages that result if change occurs. Because many of the changes being faced today by the real estate industry are truly transformational, the agents and brokers who survive must adapt new beliefs, values and behaviors. These pioneers have new mind-sets. They're open to new insights, which often provide new perspectives on old under-

FIGURE 2.2   Changes in the Real Estate Business

Things Are Changing in the Brokerage Business		
Old		**New**
Stability	CONTEXT	Change
Stable/Rising	PROFITABILITY	Declining
Primitive	TECHNOLOGY	Advanced/Changing
Managing growth	CHALLENGE	Creating growth
Semi-permanent	BROKER - AGENT RELATIONSHIPS	Transitory
Directed and paternalistic		Empowered
Commission based with proportionate split	AGENT COMPENSATION	Varied - 100% offices to salaried agents
Many desks	PRODUCTIVITY	Fewer desks/ Higher cost
Small, medium and large firms	INDUSTRY STRUCTURE	Mergers and consolidations/ disproportionate mix of large and small firms
Full-service approach business		Specialty-type firms

Reprinted with permission from the National Association of REALTORS®.

standings. When the old framework gives way to such new perspectives, a paradigm shift has occurred.

As Joel Barker so aptly states, "When the paradigm shifts, everyone goes back to zero." Our past successes guarantee nothing when the rules change, which often means that we lose our competitive advantage and chaos and turbulence reign, resulting in decreased productivity, low morale, increased tension and waning profits. Turbulence is never predictable, nor is it

FIGURE 2.2   Changes in the Real Estate Business, *continued*

Things Are Changing for Real Estate Agents		
Old		**New**
Friendly	COMPETITION	Intense
Uniformity	BUSINESS PRACTICE	Flexibility and options
Limited	TIME	Much MORE limited
General	INFORMATION	Specific, individualized
Primarily through broker-owner as teacher-mentor	EDUCATION	Education/training from variety of sources
Minimal	LIABILITY	Unlimited (buyer/seller liability, environment, disclosure)
Primary seller agent	AGENCY RELATIONSHIPS	Seller, buyer, dual non-agent facilitator
Naive	CUSTOMERS/ CLIENTS	Sophisticated
Fundamental brokerage, services - e.g., listing, management Produce in a timely fashion General knowledge	CLIENTS' EXPECTATIONS	Broad menu of "unbundled" services - e.g., marketing, financing, etc. Produce immediately Expert, accurate information

caused by (1) the failure of old paradigms, (2) attempts to prop up outmoded rules and (3) the creation and introduction of new paradigms (in turbulent times, many more paradigms will be proposed than will ever be accepted).

*S*tepping Ahead to Profit$

Reflect on the time when agency disclosure, buyer agency and then dual agency first entered your marketplace. What did you feel? How did you and your colleagues react? How do you feel about it now? Had you known then what you know now, how would you have felt and/or reacted differently?

Future Thoughts

How individuals and organizations can effectively attain/regain significant competitive advantage in such turbulent times will be discussed later in this book. But here's a clue: *The ability to anticipate can dramatically enhance your chance of success.*

Change literally affects the culture, systems, practices and processes of the real estate industry. Simultaneously, it affects the beliefs, attitudes and requisite skills of the individuals within the real estate field. Some of us react to the danger inherent in change and find ourselves in a state of paralysis. Others seize the opportunity, have flexibility and become pioneers.

CHAPTER 3

Dealing with Change

Today, dealing with change effectively means dealing with the unknown, because the rate of change is accelerating. In the past, when change was evolutionary rather than revolutionary, we could change with the environment rather than taking action to change the environment.

In the past, we were able to change on the "back side" of a wave of change because we had the luxury of time. The consequence of attempting to ride the downside of a wave—that is, simply react to what's happening in the environment—can now be expected to become more and more precarious. To deal effectively with today's changes, timing is truly everything.

Riding the Wave

If we graph a typical wave of change, dividing it into three sections (see Figure 3.1), we show the *productivity* or output per unit of resource applied (the vertical axis) against *time* (the horizontal axis). In the initial stage of any wave, discovery through experimentation is the main activity. Results are meager, and we find ourselves acting first and then developing strategies. This stage ends when the old paradigm is generally bankrupt—when applying additional resources to support the old way of doing things results in decreasing productivity.

However, those who either experiment or learn from the experiments of others will find themselves well equipped to reap the benefits during phase 2, for it is during this period that responding to challenges offers great rewards. But one must be

FIGURE 3.1   Wave of Change Graph

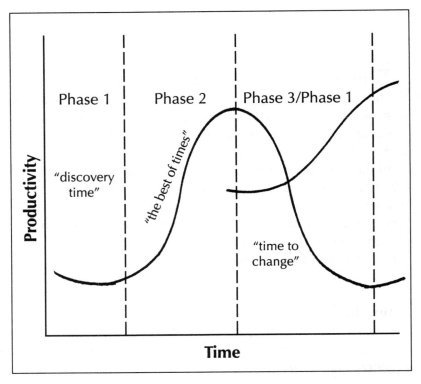

careful in applying resources (time, money, manpower) because competing paradigms exist of which one or only a few will survive and flourish. In terms of results, this is the best of times: We find ourselves doing more but also using more resources. Productivity is at its highest level, and the largest quantity of resources is applied at the peak of the curve, which is the end of phase 2.

It is in this latter portion of phase 2 that we should begin looking for new changes and new applications of "old" changes, for these can bring us into phase 1 of the next wave. This is the time to do something different, the time to change. But it is also a difficult time to change because the wave we've been riding has now achieved dominance. However, if we do nothing differently, we slide on down the back side (phase 3) of the wave. Because momentum is slowing, it takes more effort and more resources to do the same thing; in other words, we do less with more or do nothing at all (less with less).

Obviously, knowing where you are on the wave is key, but knowing which wave to "catch" is even more critical. Many changes are occurring at the same time, but only some of them offer the potential for effective solutions that yield the competitive edge. Catching an "ineffective" wave results in the inefficient expenditure of human and financial resources. Knowing which wave to ride and how to achieve the best ride requires the skills of excellence, innovation and anticipation, which we'll explore later after we understand the changes that are affecting our world and the real estate industry.

Stress and Resistance

Regardless of where you are on the wave of change, dealing with it requires recognition of the impact change has on us and our performance. The primary effect that the chaos created by change has on real estate agents and brokers is stress. Managing stress, both our own and that of people we direct, is facilitated by (1) understanding the basic reasons change is resisted and (2) instituting positive coping mechanisms for dealing with stress.

Plan or Die! 10 Keys to Organizational Success, coauthored by Timothy Nolan, Leonard Goodstein and J. William Pfeiffer, lists 22 reasons why people resist change (see Figure 3.2).

Resistance causes stress, which can result in motivation but more often results in negative emotions and behaviors—for example, anger, irritability, confusion, loss of concentration, avoidance, procrastination and even physical ailments, such as stomach and muscle aches.

To effectively diminish such effects of resistance, broker-managers should involve agents in the decision to change by making them part of the process. Use group techniques. Brainstorm about the key changes and how best to manage them, and use task forces to develop implementation details. Stress the benefits of the change so that it is perceived as happening *for* us instead of *to* us. To control rumors, management should be absolutely forthright about what's happening and keep agents informed of developments as they occur. Weekly internal newsletters/bulletins should be circulated to keep everyone current about progress and keep surprises to a bare minimum. Well-conceived plans to make changes step by step and open communication usually result in putting participants' minds at ease.

Some techniques for dealing with change are more appropriate for individuals. For example, whenever signs of stress appear, train yourself to use self-talk: Talk to others about the change and how you're reacting to it; reflect on past changes that you managed successfully; proactively learn as many specifics as possible about the change; or simply give yourself permission to take the time necessary to adjust. The critical key is to always gather more information: The more you know about the change, the better equipped you are to deal with it.

FIGURE 3.2   Reasons for Resisting Change

1. The reasons for the change have not been clearly communicated.
2. The new goals or objectives have not been accepted.
3. People fear the unknown.
4. People fear failure in a new situation.
5. People believe they prefer the present situation.
6. People have no confidence in the person proclaiming the change.
7. People support an alternative change goal.
8. People support an alternative method for implementing the change.
9. People were not involved in planning the change.
10. The proposed change will interfere with already existing plans for change.
11. The new goals are irrelevant to many people.
12. There are many different perspectives on the problem: People see the problem differently.
13. The announcement of the proposed change provides an opportunity to oppose management.
14. Accidental misstatements during the planning process set off resistance.
15. People see the proposed change as an attack on their performance.
16. People resist leaving friends and familiar surroundings.
17. Timing of the announcement is wrong.
18. People see the change as positively affecting others but see nothing for themselves.
19. People resist this change, even if it benefits them, because they fear the next change may have adverse consequences for them.
20. People fear having to learn a new job or work harder.
21. People perceive loss of status, right, or privileges because of the change.
22. People resist change simply because it is change.

Adapted from *Plan or Die! 10 Keys to Organizational Success* by T. Nolan, L. Goodstein and J.W. Pfeiffer. Copyright 1993 by Pfeiffer & Company, San Diego, Calif. Used with permission.

*S*tepping Ahead to Profit$

Make two lists of the major changes you have experienced in the past 12 months, one for changes in your business and one for personal changes. Select the most important (or interesting, fun, etc.) change from each list. Reflect on your reaction to each change: How did you feel? Was it a real surprise or did you have a hunch it was coming? What events led you to anticipate the change? What did you do as a result of each change? How did you do it? Using 20:20 hindsight, should you have done things differently? If so, how? Why? Given what you've learned from this exercise, how can you prepare for future change so that stress and disruption are minimized?

Future Thoughts

Dealing with change requires effective and careful management of both ourselves and others. Understanding that changes in the environment about us occur predictably in waves helps us to visualize and therefore better implement responsive changes within our businesses and industry.

Because most humans respond to change with resistance, we need to understand more specifically why people resist. To effectively diminish the results of such resistance, broker-managers and individual agents should use positive coping mechanisms, including techniques to develop shared vision/understanding, rumor control, learning as much as possible about the change and open discussion.

PART TWO

Changing Trends in American Business

CHAPTER 4

The Changing Social and Economic Environment

Change is hard, and sometimes we feel ill-equipped to handle it. The world that is changing so much around us and is challenging the real estate business is one in which the middle—the "glue" to the entire American experience—is disappearing.

The vanishing middle is significant, and we see it all over. We see it internationally when the news focuses on nationalistic rebellions, like the one that recently faced the Russians in Chechnya—a place that most of us never knew existed and probably have no real concept of still.

We see it in politics. The election of 1994 took a real toll on the middle. The Republicans who leaned toward the right swept the Congress, but the Democrats who won were the ones who tended toward the left, not the moderates.

We see it in our own cities and towns as well. Recently a 14-year-old high school freshman in Washington shot and killed a sophomore after an argument about a girl. All of us (especially the males), when we were teenagers, got into that kind of argument, and occasionally it came to blows. Now it doesn't come to blows, it comes to bullets.

The erosion in the middle is important because the country and the real estate industry are built on the middle. An erosion of that middle—polarization of the economy and society—is going to be a major problem for American democracy and real estate as well.

The disappearance of the middle occurs gradually and marginally, but even marginal changes have tremendous impact. Take housing, for example. We have 100 million dwelling units in this country. In a good year, 5 percent of that stock turns over in sales transactions. If that 5 percent becomes 4 percent, that represents 20 percent of the real estate brokerage business. How many of you would not look upon a 20 percent reduction in your business as a disaster? So, even though marginal changes make up our history, we need to look at them with a perspective that accurately assesses their true impact.

Three Views of the Middle

Let's look at this vanishing middle in three categories, each of which has significance for the real estate business: the economy, demographics and everybody's favorite subject, technology. In each category, the changes have both a positive and a negative potential. Nothing is so foreordained that it moves only in one direction. It can be more positive and less negative, or more negative and less positive, but everything has two sides.

The Economy

The growth factor.   Three things are going to determine what happens in the economy over the next 10–15 years. The first is *slow growth*. We are not going to see any consistent period of boom, and a real growth rate of about 2.5 percent is probably a good guess for the balance of this decade and the first decade of the 21st century.

There are a couple of reasons for that. One of them sits at the helm of the Fed. Alan Greenspan is firmly convinced that 2.5 percent is an appropriate and sustainable growth rate, and he is going to try to keep it close to that. More important, one of the major engines of the economy for the past 50 years is slowing down and going out of service, and that is the government.

The election of 1994 is a symptom rather than a cause. Over the next two decades, expect to see less government at the federal level. Both the Republicans and the Democrats are vigorously advocating its downsizing. With the Congress, it's easy to dismiss this as so much rhetoric. But scaling down government was one of the major themes of the Clinton-Gore campaign of 1992, and they'll likely return to it in 1996.

In many cases, this talk has become reality: Government, both military and civilian, is becoming smaller. As it does, it will be less of a driving positive force on the economy than it has been at any point since the end of World War II—certainly since the end of the Korean War. This is a reality that we need to adapt to and live with.

There are positives and negatives about a shrinking government. The negative side, obviously, is that the government is a major consumer—and whenever you reduce consumption, you reduce economic activity as a whole. It's also a major employer. So when the government downsizes, the whole economy suffers.

The upside of that, of course, is that the government, because of its continuing budget deficit, absorbs a lot of resources in the form of private savings that could be used for other purposes— for example, homebuying.

The inflation factor.   The second economic trend is *low inflation*. There is really no inflation in this economy, and there is unlikely to be any for four main reasons.

First, the demographics of the labor force argue against it. The bulk of the American population is at an age where saving for retirement or paying big expenditures for education or for housing are major concerns. That will reduce consumption in other areas.

Second, we have changed drastically in the way in which we consume things. Every time you walk into a Warehouse Club, an outlet or some similar "category buster," what are you doing? You are basically going for low-cost, no-frills services and goods. In other words, more and more goods are being purchased at prices below retail. Because the Consumer Price Index uses retail prices, inflation is actually less than the number announced by the Labor Department each month.

Third, we have seen a resurgence of private labels. When I was growing up, we used to buy supermarket label goods because that was what we could afford. When you bought supermarket label goods, you got watery soup and canned vegetables that were mostly liquid and did not taste very good. Now when you buy private labels you get quality that is roughly the equivalent of brand names. Not because the brands are worse, but because private labels are better. That cuts down prices.

Fourth, and in part because of the competition represented by the last two factors, there has been a general "toughening up" within a corporate sector that cannot pass along price increases. Add to this the fact that corporations have now gone to labor practices that allow them to do "just in time" labor. What is needed for a day is hired for a day—no benefits, no obligations, no extra cost built in.

All these factors are going to put a lid on inflation and put it on very dramatically. But lower inflation also has two sides. Generally, lower inflation makes planning easier and life more dependable. In Switzerland, the prices of canned goods are printed on the labels at the factory. They are not applied at the supermarket. They are not in little slots under the shelves. They are not captured in a computer bar code whose value could be changed. That is what low inflation does; it gives you a sense of security. It stabilizes the economy and it stabilizes society. I think we have seen over the years that high inflation is as much of a political destabilizer as it is an economic destabilizer.

The downside, of course, is that low inflation doesn't make real property very attractive as an investment. Those who own or are selling real property have a vested, personal interest in higher inflation. Low inflation means less turnover and less demand for real property.

Income disparity. The third economic fact of life is income disparity. If you look at the data, it is very clear that the income distribution in the United States is widening. Most professionals think it will continue that way. The amount of income controlled by the top 10 percent of earners has increased at the expense of the bottom 10 percent.

The jobs we are creating either pay handsomely, because they are knowledge-based, or they barely pay at all, because they are semiskilled. There is not much in between. This is far different from the 1950s, when the postwar economic boom was based on the creation of steady, union jobs in manufacturing. The assembly-line image and the middle-class suburban society connected to it have been built into our economic mythology, but the trend has changed. Manufacturing jobs that create middle-class homes and middle-class households aren't being created anymore. The polarization of the income distribution is both an indicator and a result of this change.

Think about the consequences for specific kinds of businesses. For example, Sears is a middle-class retailer. It cannot move down the income scale, because that market has been captured by the Walton empire and the big warehouse discounters. It cannot move up, because nobody is going to believe that Sears is of the same quality as, say, a Nordstrom. Sears is boxed in and its client base is shrinking.

So if you examine this income polarization from the viewpoint of Sears, you're unhappy. But if you look at it from the viewpoint of somebody else—Wal-Mart, Nordstrom—you feel pretty good about it because the market is coming to you. So, again, there are good sides and bad sides.

Real estate is a lot like Sears. If you think about it, home sales is a middle-class business. The bulk of residential sales is clustered within 10 percent of the median price in any market. Middle-income households buy and sell these homes. If the clientele in that market begins to shrink, there may be just as many sales, but they will be at lower prices, and maybe for the same houses. Senator Alan Cranston once said, "The good thing about inflation is that it lets you live in a better neighborhood—even if you don't move." A shrinking middle class could generate the opposite result. So, there is a possible downside.

As you can see, the primary characteristics of this economy—slow growth, low inflation and income disparity—will have both positive and negative influences on the real estate business.

$\mathcal{S}$tepping Ahead to Profit$

Are you Wal-Mart or Sears or Nordstrom's? Write down your primary business goal and then exactly how slow growth, low inflation and income polarization are helping you reach that goal or are keeping you from it. Is your market better or worse than the nation as a whole? List those differences. Do they make it harder or easier for you to do business?

Demographics

George Will once noted that in a democracy, demography is destiny. Right now there are three demographic trends shaping up that will transform American society and the economy over the next 25 years.

We're getting older. By the year 2010, one out of every five Americans will be over the age of 65. We are getting old with the baby boom generation, that outburst of births between 1946 and 1964. That group has dominated American culture and the economy in every phase of its life. While it was being born, we built highways and suburbs and schools and hospitals; when it reached adolescence, social disruption was the norm; in the '70s when it left college, the result was a huge, inexperienced labor force that led to persistent stagflation; in the '80s, as it matured, the economy boomed on the basis of its spending.

The baby boom generation will also dominate American society and culture in its next phase of life. The positive side is that we are going to see a significant shift in the demand for real estate. This will not simply be a shift in volume—in fact, sales volume may be greater—but also a shift in nature. *The biggest client group will become the resizer, the over-55 household looking to move into its last house.* This will be an attractive client base. It is going to be an affluent generation, one that is used to making its own decisions. The market will clearly shift into that area by the end of the century.

The downside of the aging population is that we are setting ourselves up, with the right set of circumstances, for extreme social polarization to accompany the income polarization we discussed earlier in this chapter. By and large, the baby boomers have been a socially aware and involved generation. Will these folks move into more appropriate housing in their town and remain as committed and as active and involved as they have in the past? Or, will they retreat to a gated community someplace where they can associate with people of their own kind and insulate themselves from the world outside?

Older Americans vote in higher-than-average percentages and tend to be single-issue voters. When the hard questions about downsizing government are finally faced and Social Security is on the table, will senior citizens exert their will to the detriment of the rest of society? And how would that affect social relations in this country? This is a question that is going to have a lot to do with shaping the society we will inhabit in the future.

Most first-time buyers will be foreign-born.   If the real estate market shifts toward the resizers, where will the first-time buyers come from? Here we encounter the second demographic trend. The biggest portion of the first-time buyer market will be accounted for by immigration. In 1992 *one-third* of all U.S. net population growth was accounted for by immigration.

One of the things that we know about groups that have legally immigrated in the past is that their home-ownership rates increase dramatically. Between 1980 and 1990, home-ownership rates for every native-born American group in the prime homebuying ages went down. Home ownership for every immigrant group in the same age ranges went up.

For those who immigrated to this country before 1979, there was a marginal increase in home-ownership rates. Home-ownership rates for those who immigrated after 1979 go from 30 percent to 45 percent—and this pattern is continuing. These are highly motivated groups. They are coming here for a reason, and part of it—perhaps the major part—is the good old American dream, home ownership.

Now let's talk about the upsides and downsides of that. The upside is that, as they have in the past, immigrant groups bring new ideas and new energy. They tend to be the best of their generation. My grandfather walked over a hill, got on a boat and went off to the United States without a lot of understanding of what he would face. When he got here, he went to work for an ice house and wound up running the business. He had never worked in that business or run any business before. Those who come to the United States are the most courageous of their group, and they have historically added to this country new bursts of energy and ideas.

American families are changing.   The final demographic trend is the changing structure of American families. One of the most significant events of 1994 may have been the death of Harriet Nelson. Ozzie and Harriet Nelson represented the traditional American family, the married-with-children household. In fact, when Ozzie and Harriet were on TV, 75 percent of all American families were married couples with children.

Clearly, that image no longer reflects reality. Even by the 1970s, the popular culture family of record was the Bradys, a blended suburban household. But even that has changed, and changed dramatically: By the year 2000, that category will constitute only 46 percent of American families. Increasingly, American households are single individuals, single parents (increasingly with both their children *and* their parents), unmarried couples and groups.

All this, of course, could change again, and there are some indications that it might. Culturally, we are swinging to the conservative side, with a prominent national dialogue over values, including family values. As a matter of fact, we are now seeing in very small numbers—not yet a trend, but a ripple on the water—one parent in a young, professional household drop-ping out of the labor force to stay home and take care of and instill values in the kids. Some yuppies have ceased being yuppies and have become what are now being called SITCOMs—Single Income, Two Children, Oppressive Mortgage.

All these changes offer new challenges to people in the real estate community. Households live in houses; they buy them and they sell them. The successful real estate practitioner must be prepared to deal with a variety of client and customer ar-rangements, and to understand that every client is going to have different needs. The married couple with young children may be attracted to a neighborhood by its school system, but good schools will not even appear on the radar screen of a single person, or even an unmarried couple.

What is the upside and the downside? The upside here is the strength that America has always drawn from its diversity. A range of family and household types promotes the kind of toler-ance and interaction that generates social harmony. We may no longer be Ozzie and Harriet, or even the Brady Bunch. But we can realize that households and homeowners, no matter what their configuration, build solid values and make this country great.

$\mathcal{S}$tepping Ahead to Profit$

Make a list of all the clients and customers you've dealt with in the past six months. Where do they fit demographi-cally? Make a similar list from three and five years ago. How do these lists compare? Ask your colleagues (particularly those who have been in the business longer than you) what their experience has been.

Technology

You can read *The Wall Street Journal, USA Today, The New York Times* or even your local paper any day and you will find a story about technology. In a great many cases the stories report brand new, not yet fully developed devices, and you probably won't hear of or use them for quite awhile. Does that mean you should ignore them as some kind of sci-fi speculation? No. Ninety-five percent of those stories are speculative. The inventions and breakthroughs described will help your business only long after you've forgotten the story ever appeared.

Let me give you a personal example. In 1971, I wrote a Ph.D. dissertation on the impact of electronic banking on monetary flows within the economy. At that time, predictions of a "cashless society" were rampant. We were going to have "smart" cards and wouldn't need to carry cash or credit cards or have checking accounts. Rather, we would have a single card that would execute all our transactions. It didn't happen in 1968, or in 1978, and in fact it is just happening now—25 years later. That is a long gestation period, but it is going to happen.

The key point here is that gestation periods for technological innovations are shrinking. Those born in the 1940s remember— vividly—the first time they saw a TV. Yet that same group has trouble remembering their first experience with a cellular phone or a VCR or a fax machine. The innovations are coming thicker and faster: Today's idea is tomorrow's sale item at the consumer electronics store (see Figure 1.2, page 6).

Human transmission becomes obsolete.   What does technology do? To begin with, it replaces people who don't add value. We've already seen this in action. The recession of 1990– 91 began in the financial services sector and in the Northeast. The application of technology on a wide scale in that sector resulted in the redundancy of middle management—people whose job consisted of gathering information and passing it on to other people. It is done electronically much more easily, quickly and efficiently.

This trend will continue and reach deep into the production process, because the technological curve leads to more power in smaller packages for less cost. This chapter is being "written" on a laptop computer. That machine has more computational power than existed electronically on the entire planet in 1960. The trend toward electronic transmission replacing human transmission will thus not only continue but also reach into smaller and smaller economic units as the price of progress falls.

Global cottage industries emerge. Secondly, technology produces whole new business arrangements. A friend of mine recently got into agricultural consulting, even though he had never been near a farm in his life. He realized that growing crops give off certain wavelengths of infrared light at different stages of growth and that these waves could be detected in satellite photos. So, he bought satellite computer images sorted for the proper light-wave values and began advising potato farmers in Oregon where and when to plant to take over the winter potato market from Idaho. And he did it all without leaving Oklahoma.

In his latest career shift, he's advising the government of Szechwan Province, China, in the establishment of gambling casinos, which he will monitor electronically from Oklahoma. This may seem far removed from potato farming, but the constant of technological innovation makes such shifts eminently logical.

Supply and demand connect "just in time." Technology streamlines production and labor processes. One of the major advances made by the Japanese auto industry in the 1970s was the creation of "just in time" inventory. Rather than store glass, sheet metal, paint, tires and all the other compound parts, sophisticated software allows direct connection with suppliers, so that production schedules are matched and inventory costs absolutely minimized.

This theory applies to labor as well. A recent article in *Fortune* dealt with the future of work. It centered around the idea that many American workers now view themselves as bundles of capacity ("just in time" inventory) that can be applied at a variety of firms, and even in a variety of industries. Increasingly, labor value is less tied to experience with a specific company, but rather to that bundle of competency and how it fits with modern business needs. The concept is quite familiar to the real estate business, because the independent contractor has been the backbone of the business for years. Success comes from the combination of the brokerage infrastructure with the bundle of competency that is the salesperson.

Changing Perceptions of Value

As technological change moves us to a knowledge-based society and economy, our view of the relative value of assets changes as well—a change that may affect real estate. In *The Age of Paradox*, Charles Handy describes nine paradoxes in society, one being the "paradox of intelligence." He writes:

> As a small indicator of the changing perception of property, we may observe that the richer we are, the less we seem to feel the need to own our own homes. In Bangladesh 90 percent of the houses are owner-occupied. In Ireland 82 percent. In rich Germany, the western part, the figure falls to 45 percent. In richer Switzerland it is only 33 percent. *Where brains prevail, security lies not in physical property, but in the intelligence quotient. There are then better uses for cash than buying houses.* (Emphasis added)

Economic, demographic and technological trends that are sweeping society are marginal but significant. They are not going to affect everybody in the world. But a change that creates even a small differential can have huge effects for specific sectors. If a trend—such as the primacy of intellectual assets over physical, for example—reduces the home-ownership rate by one percentage point, it wipes out 20 percent of the real estate business. Trends, when they are real, are extremely important.

Now, let's hook these trends—economic, demographic, technological—together and apply them at the national level. Over the past two decades, we have moved into an unfamiliar place in the world economy: outside looking in at the Germans, the Japanese and a few other folks. If we are again to become a leader in the knowledge-based world economy, we must make the necessary investment from our own resources. Will we have the capacity to make those investments? How do long-term trends affect that capacity? How does that play out with the federal deficit? Is a deficit caused by the investment necessary to keep us on top as a knowledge-based economy justified in some sense?

We start with a handicap because the vehicle we have always used for national investment, namely the defense budget, is disappearing. Think about how we invest as a nation. You may not remember this, but our great interstate highway system was funded under the National Defense Highway Act. We built the highways ostensibly to evacuate our cities in the case of nuclear attack. When we produced a great number of Ph.D.s during the late 1960s and 1970s, we funded these budding academics through the National Defense Education Act. We trained our youth to compete with the Soviet science establishment.

So, you have to ask, are we going to be able to step up to the plate and make these kinds of investments, the deficit be damned? Or, do we balance the budget at all costs, and throw the baby out with the bath water? What will happen? What will the impact be? Where do we go from there? We know that the society that will deal with those questions is emerging from the demographic and technological forces described above. And the answers will drive this economy for the next century.

Future Thoughts

The future is by no means set. In fact, in a world where an increasing rate of change in all aspects of life is the norm, perhaps there are no set answers at all.

Americans love to say, "I love to change. Change is my thing. I am always changing. I am dynamic." It is almost part of the national consciousness. What we really mean is "I want that guy over there to change, and I'm going to sit here and watch." Be conscious of that. As you process all the facts and opinions that swirl about you in the evolving future, remember that *change is not a spectator sport.*

CHAPTER 5

The New Realities of American Business

At the beginning of this century, eight of the ten largest companies in the United States were related to natural resource extraction and conversion, and one of every ten British workers was a coal miner. At the end of the century, the major growth industries are microelectronics, biotechnology, the new materials sciences, telecommunications, aviation manufacturing, machine tools and robotics, and computer software and hardware. It's not important that you be able to recognize and explain any of these; but it is important that you recognize their essential reliance on workers' knowledge and brain power.

The evolution of major economic activity across the 20th century speaks volumes about the way in which our world has changed. We have moved from manufacturing based on natural resources to manufacturing using synthetic materials, to services, to knowledge as the basis for our economy. In doing so, we have created a mobile, rootless society in which no business must locate in a specific place (e.g., steel mills in Pittsburgh, where the raw materials could be assembled efficiently). Television is the information source, and electronic forums are the town square. In short, *we exist in time, but increasingly less in space.*

If you had opened the business pages of your local papers as recently as ten years ago, you probably would not have encountered any of the following topics in any of the stories:

- Nikkei Index
- Empowerment
- Virtual reality
- Workplace diversity
- Fiber optics
- Total quality management
- W. Edwards Deming
- Strategic alliances

The fact that they are now unavoidable says a great deal about how the thinking of American business has changed—sometimes by choice and sometimes by necessity.

Unfortunately, technology changes much faster than do the mental models that govern the course of business. Those models remain unexamined and unquestioned even though, assailed by the constant stress and change of the past decade, they succeed less and less as reliable guides to business strategy.

Winning in the Competitive Global Environment

In the wake of a shrinking, changing world market, businesses have been forced away from a mental model characterized by allegiance to the status quo ("What's good for General Motors is good for America!") toward a marketing mentality that emphasizes efficiency and recognizes the primacy of customers' needs in a dynamic marketplace. Consider the words of Jack

Welch, CEO of General Electric and one of the most visionary and committed business executives in America today:

> We run General Electric on a simple premise: The only way to win, in the brutally competitive global environment in which we operate, is to get more output from less input in all 12 of our businesses and, by doing so, become the lowest-cost producer of high-quality goods and services in the world.

This is not a statement that would have been made in 1950, when American business was king of the hill, or in 1970, when the world was just beginning to draw closer together economically, but it resonates with the realities of the 1990s, when the need to compete globally on the basis of product quality and customer service drives the marketplace. (By the way, GE is the only company that survives from those ten top companies of 1900 mentioned at the beginning of this chapter.)

Now, American business increasingly defines the market as larger than the United States, identifies the customer by needs rather than gender or race and serves a household far different from that of Ozzie and Harriet.

$\mathcal{S}$tepping Ahead to Profit$

What is your mental model for your business? Write your vision in 55 words or less. Print it out in big, bold type and put it on the wall near your desk. Read it daily. As you finish reading each chapter of this book, you may find you want to make changes to your vision. If you do, don't hesitate to revise it.

Like most shifts in mind-set, the adjustment of American business did not happen overnight, yet the realization that our paradigms needed renovation was triggered by a single, highly visible process. For years, the nuclear family has been shrinking as a portion of all households. And for years, new inventions have brought us ever closer to that carrot of technology that has seemingly dangled just out of our reach. But all these developments were like a coral reef that grows slowly and imperceptibly beneath the surface of the water.

The reef broke the surface with the rise to world dominance of the Japanese and German economies during the 1980s. Suddenly, American business, so used to holding first place in the world economy, held not first, not second, but *third* place in the new world economic order. And we were falling behind not because of size—we still were larger than either of our major competitors—but because of technique: The Japanese (especially) and the Germans did things differently from us. They not only worked differently, their fundamental assumptions—their mental models—about business were different. If American business were to catch up, it had to change the way it thought about business.

The Mighty U.S. Auto Industry Stumbles ... and Recovers

Perhaps nowhere has this change been more evident than in the automobile industry. Subscribing to beliefs that the consumer could be dictated to (as Henry Ford put it: "You can have any color car you want, as long as it's black"); that style, not quality or reliability, was the only important consideration; and that the industry could be run by top-down management, American manufacturers were demolished by foreign products in the 1980s. They failed to see that technology and management technique were passing them by and that their customers were changing.

The initial reaction to foreign competition was protection-ism—"Buy American" campaigns and appeals to Congress to raise tariffs—but the American public always puts its pocket-book where its needs are met, and those tactics failed. Eventu-ally, Detroit began listening to customers, using technology to create better vehicles and cooperating with foreign producers rather than simply fighting them.

The result has been a remarkable comeback for American automobile makers, both firms and workers. The quality of U.S.-made cars is now comparable to that of Japanese automobiles and maybe even ahead of other countries, and we lead the world in light-truck production. More important, these vehicles are produced in an environment in which robotics are effec-tively employed, line workers can make essential decisions about quality implementation, factories control costs through modern inventory management and *design is based on what customers need, rather than what the manufacturer thinks they should have.*

The story of the automobile industry has all the elements of the general shift in mental models that is now affecting Ameri-can business, including the real estate industry.

- Technology has increased the spread of information, the speed of communication and the flexibility of production.
- It has allowed for more participative management and con-trol of some aspect of the business process by all levels of an organization.
- Better-informed consumers have the power to demand that their increasingly diverse needs are met by businesses.
- In a more interdependent world, insularity and territoriality are losing strategies; thus is created the necessary compe-tition to assure that consumer preferences can be imple-mented.

In the following sections, we explore how people and tech-nology have driven these changes and how they are changing the mental models used by American firms. For each, we identify a selection of new beliefs that are governing American business, particularly as they pertain to real estate. We do not attempt to be comprehensive here; rather, we describe the root causes of the shifts and discuss a few of them to create a context for our later analysis of specific changes that significantly affect the real estate business. The real estate business is coming late to some of these changes, but it must adapt to them if it is to remain viable in the future.

People Trends: Older, Wiser and More Demanding

Markets are shifting. Consumption trends are increasingly dominated by older buyers, while the work force is increasingly younger and more comfortable with technology. Immigration, in numbers unseen for nearly a century, is a significant feature on the economic landscape, and Americans who are living longer than anyone (including themselves) expected are a concern for American business and for public policy.

Since 1950, every major trend in the American economy, and society in general, has been driven by the presence of the baby boom generation. We built hospitals where they could be born, suburbs so their parents could raise them well and schools so they could become educated. When they were teens, they were responsible for a youth revolution that was amazing both in its capacity for social disruption and in its power to shape production and consumption. When they reached a degree of maturity, they flooded the labor market and produced a stagflation that was unprecedented in the economy. When their skills and income caught up, they led a consumption boom that powered the 1980s.

Now they are older, affluent and thinking about the second half of their lives. During their entire existence, their needs constituted the dominant element of both public policy and private businesses. They expect that catering to continue and have transferred their expectations into the marketplace through a demand for nothing less than perfect customer service.

Work styles are changing as well. With the resizing of American industry, there has been a dramatic increase in the part-time and temporary work force. In addition, those cut loose from giant enterprises are increasingly redefining themselves as consultants and information integrators, who provide the backup and support to the primary manufacturers of products and providers of services. They work where they live and feel less and less loyalty to large organizations.

Compounding all this, the boomer generation is sandwiched between their parents, who are outliving their resources and relying on their children for survival, and their own children, who are caught in a changing economy in which values are crumbling and careers are hard to find. Because of all these considerations, the impact of boomers on society will be no less in the coming decade than it was in the past four decades. From this flow seven new business paradigms that are essential to the real estate industry.

1. Successful Businesses Will Excel in Customer Service

Boeing.   Early in 1994, Boeing rolled out its newest model, the 777, a wide-bodied, technologically current, highly flexible commercial passenger jet. For the first time, the design and construction process of the airplane included substantial and significant input from the customer side. For three years, United Airlines, the major purchaser of the plane, provided a team of its employees to work beside Boeing engineers. Additionally, Boeing regularly conducted focus groups and other types of discussions with flight personnel to ensure that the design of the plane incorporated the elements that they valued as users and that they saw as enhancing passenger satisfaction.

Ritz-Carlton.   Annually, the highest-rated hotel chain in the United States is Ritz-Carlton. In fact, the company has received the Baldrige award for quality. One of the keys to the success of Ritz-Carlton is its empowerment of employees to guarantee customer satisfaction. Whenever a guest has a need or a problem, any employee, from the facility manager to the cleaning staff, is *entitled and expected* to leave what he or she is doing and solve that customer's need. The result is a perception that Ritz-Carlton values its customers above all else.

One example represents the manufacturing side of the economy, the other the service sector, but both are symptomatic of what's going on throughout American business. Wal-Mart has become a major American success story by combining two critical consumer keys in its policy of low prices and knowledgeable customer service. Even Nordstrom, the upscale retailer, has succeeded despite higher prices by establishing a reputation for peerless customer service, to the point where the firm's CEO has been known to personally call customers who have a problem and work with them to solve the issue. The bottom line here is that *no firm that deals with either products or services can afford not to specialize in excellent customer service.*

This particular mental mind-set creates a process, not a destination. Customer service expectations grow as that service is delivered, so that stakes go up continually. Think about real estate. Customers' expectations of speed and accuracy have gone up as technology has allowed the real estate transaction to be completed faster and more efficiently, congruent with increased transaction complexity. As technological sophistication grows, the better real estate firms will implement new methods and raise the standards of doing business. Those firms unable to match those standards will fall by the wayside.

***S*tepping Ahead to Profit$**

Think about your firm. Have you and your associates developed a habit of excellence in customer service? List five ideas that can move you toward even better customer service, and describe how you will implement them over the next six months.

2. Workers Respond Productively to a System of Individual Responsibility and Accountability

The current labor force, dominated as it is by the baby-boom generation, has been conditioned by a social structure that allows workers to influence matters that affect their lives. In the workplace, this has translated into the ability to directly affect the production process. To a great extent, this has come out of the Japanese model of delegation that has proven so competitively successful.

General Electric.   Jack Welch at General Electric has been a leader in this change. GE is characterized by a great deal of individual autonomy over production decisions and management, which stimulates the real participation of the labor force. Moreover, individual units of the corporation have planning and execution authority over production processes. But the process of adapting to this mind-set is long and hard. It requires a full cultural change within the organization that, Welch estimates for GE, can take five to ten years. The good news here is that most real estate firms are smaller, and thus the process will be shorter. The bad news is that real estate firms have never paid much attention to organizational development issues and thus must acquire some very basic skills.

---

*S*tepping Ahead to Profit$

How would you describe the culture of your firm? Is it participatory? Does it allow for good, profitable ideas to flow through from all areas of the company? If not, how would you change the culture so that the entire firm is open to growth and profitability?

Saturn.   The automobile industry is perhaps an even better example. Saturn, a joint venture of General Motors and Nissan, is produced through a process that incorporates teamwork and individual accountability. Instead of on an assembly line, Saturns are manufactured by teams that bear responsibility for all aspects of production, including recommending and implementing changes in the process that will allow for more efficiency. National advertising for Saturn even emphasizes this arrangement, with a particularly effective TV spot centering on a thank-you note from a schoolteacher to the team that actually made her new car.

The shift from hierarchical organizational forms to decentralized cooperative ventures may have resulted from the pressure of Japanese competition, and in the automotive industry this was probably the case. But the majority of the labor force came to maturity in the 1960s, when the ideas of individual freedom, cooperative action and open debate ingrained themselves into the American consciousness. They have now surfaced in the workplace and are ignored by businesses only at their own risk.

3. Consumers Are Becoming Increasingly Sophisticated

The New York Times recently ran a story about the difficulty most advertisers are having reaching "Generation X," the post-boomers who are now reaching their economic independence and maturity. This generation, raised on television, has been exposed to enough hype to be able to separate the steak from the sizzle.

More important, all consumers are becoming accustomed to receiving information electronically. This means that businesses must now pay as much attention to the medium as the message—witness the importance for the advertising community of the Superbowl, which has become less a football game than a festival of new-product pitches. To add to this, one national newspaper, *USA Today*, rates these ads through panel reactions and provides the results the next day, using only slightly less space than is devoted to the game report.

With these changes, consumers have become more impatient with slow and protracted messages, responding better to the quick image—visual methods best exemplified by music videos and MTV. This technique has been adapted in the more successful TV ads and is becoming increasingly apparent in print advertising.

But besides paying more attention to the sizzle, consumers are also eating more steak. The amount of information available to consumers has expanded dramatically. Whether through online computer networks, the growth of consumer advocacy groups or simply the more detailed materials flowing from manufacturers, most consumers know more about products than they have at any time in history.

To sell, a product (or a salesperson) must captivate the individual's "learning channel." In addition to a change in the nature of those channels, they are also carrying much heavier loads. This is significant for most businesses, but especially critical to firms that trade in information. *And real estate firms trade in information.*

$\mathcal{S}$tepping Ahead to Profit$

Look at your company's approach to advertising. What age and demographic groups does it "grab"? Are these the groups that make up the bulk of your effective market? How can you adjust if this is not the case?

Technology: Changing the Rate of Change

This has been a bad decade for control freaks, particularly of the political variety. The actual fall of the Berlin Wall in 1989 touched off the symbolic fall of the Communist monolith in the following years. The once-mighty Soviet empire, with its republics and vassal states, now exists only as the historical partner to Rome. The tightly orchestrated regimes of Asia, from the totalitarian Chinese state to the guided "democracy" of Singapore, are finding it increasingly difficult to stifle opposing voices. Even in the United States, the discipline that created the two-party system has dissolved to the point where the independent electoral effort of Ross Perot captured 18 percent of the national vote in 1992, and no issue in the Congress can be predicted simply on party-line voting.

The common denominator here is the impact of technology in making information accessible. Without the free flow of information through electronic channels, the restlessness that brought down the centralized states of Eastern Europe would never have developed. Without the ability to communicate through the uncontrolled channels provided by computer networks, organized opposition to any regime can be easily stamped out. Without direct and effective access to the information pools that drive public policy, legislators would still be subject to party controls.

The body of information and the channels of communication available to every individual have expanded exponentially in the past decade and will continue to do so. Think about your own situation. Can you do business today without a fax machine? A cellular phone? A PC networked to an information source? Probably not. But ten years ago, even five years ago, your business world, and the tools that service it, were completely different. And there is no way you can envision how you will conduct your business five years from now. Unfortunately, because those five years will pass in a wink, you must try to form that picture.

Technology is changing how we do things, and at a more rapid rate all the time. Remember the example of how many people could tell the exact moment when they first saw television, but were hazy on more modern innovations? This occurs because momentous developments such as television once happened only occasionally and thus had a large impact on our consciousness. Now, those innovations come so quickly and in such large numbers that they seem almost commonplace.

But innovation means more than just an increase in the supply of "toys." The real impact has been the change in the manner in which businesses, particularly those that either deal directly in or rely heavily on information, view their relationships with their customers. That means a shift in the mental models we all have for our businesses.

4. *Each Firm Focuses on Only One Customer at a Time*

Bar code scanners have proven to be a real time saver in American supermarkets. Although greeted with skepticism at first, they have significantly reduced the amount of time one stands in line waiting to pay for one's groceries. If they did only that, they would have been worth the price. But savvy merchandisers have integrated scanners as information-gathering devices that have allowed them to personalize their relationship with their customers.

Publix. A particularly striking example of this is Publix supermarkets, a Florida chain. Like so many other food stores, Publix issues check-cashing and discount cards to its customers. When a customer goes through the checkout line, the store's computers record each purchase, and over time a portrait of that customer's buying habits emerges. Additionally, the customer's Social Security number allows this information to be combined with other databases collected by other retailers and public agencies to create an even more thorough picture of the consuming household.

Publix can now use this information to target mailings directly to the individual customer—for example, a packet of coupons covering those products most often used by the household. The image is of a retailer who speaks directly to the customer, establishing a strong tie and increased loyalty. By the way, when the customer uses the coupons, more information is added to the database.

Smart retailers everywhere, realizing that the best marketing approach is one that singles out the customer and personalizes the relationship, are using technology to custom tailor the product to the individual. Publix is looking to be the *only* supermarket in the customer's life. In the real estate industry, this customized approach has appeared in the form of specific and personalized listing presentations and the use of databases to integrate property and neighborhood information into a total package. In the future, as more sophisticated systems come online, the customization process will increasingly focus on the individualized needs of both buyer and seller.

$\mathcal{S}$tepping Ahead to Profit$

Draw up an ideal plan that would result in approaching only those with whom you have a 75 percent or greater probability of successfully completing a transaction. How does that differ from what you do now? How can you move toward this ideal?

---

5. The Consumer Controls Marketing

If you've ever traveled, you've probably stayed in a hotel with in-room movies, probably provided through Spectravision. The movies were a bit more expensive, but new enough not to be available even on cable, and you could watch them in the privacy and comfort of your hotel room. The hitch was that the movies ran only at specified times: If you checked in at 10:15 PM and "Batman Forever" was playing at 10 and midnight, your choice was to miss part of the movie or fight to stay awake to see it fully. The price of the movie made this an unappealing choice. Two years ago, Spectravision introduced Viewer's Choice, a system that allowed a guest to call up a movie, in its entirety, at the guest's convenience. In hotels where this service existed, Spectravision's revenues soared.

In 1985, $12 billion was spent by Americans in telephone merchandise orders. In 1995, that number will be $57 billion. If you think about it, this is not a terribly effective way of buying:

You can't try it on, you can't take it home with you and you can't feel or actually see the goods—only pictures. But (and this is a huge factor in a world of two-earner households where the only scarcity is time) you *can* shop at three in the morning, or on an airplane, or while you're in your pajamas.

These two examples typify an emerging trend in business: *Customers will buy when, where and how it pleases them.* Technology has multiplied the channels through which information flows in our society, and has personalized those channels to the point where consumers can choose the messages they receive and the timing of those messages. Cable television is a prominent example of this, giving the viewer the opportunity to tune away from the broadcast messages of the major networks and choose instead from a variety of specialized programming that is, if not commercial free, lighter on advertising. In the future, as cable expands to hundreds of channels, individuals will have the power to create a single customized channel that will carry only the messages (programming and advertising) that they wish to receive.

Additionally, as use of the World Wide Web increases, more and more companies are creating their own information "home pages" to carry information about their products. This, of course, only reinforces the trend, as the page cannot be read unless the consumer chooses to bring it up on the screen.

For real estate professionals, the implications here are enormous, and we talk about them in detail in the next chapter. However, suffice it to say here that the real estate business has been built on the foundation of preferential access to, and special expertise in, information about property. The technology that puts the consumer in control weakens that foundation and equalizes the market power of agent and customer.

$\mathcal{S}$tepping Ahead to Profit$

Assume that three years from now, the consumer has complete access to all property information. What services will you offer in the marketplace? How will you price them? How will you promote them? Draw up the outline of a business plan for that world.

---

6. Firms Are Information Consultants

Among its other advantages, a compact disc (CD) player allows the listener to move smoothly to specific tracks on specific discs. This enables the consumer, especially one with a multidisc player, to customize a sequence of selections and, in effect, create her own concert. This capability fits in quite well with the new mental models described above.

Each track on a CD is preceded by a piece of information describing the artist and the selection, coded in a form readable by a laser beam. The player knows where Barbra Streisand is singing "Evergreen" and where to go to get Jimi Hendrix's version of the national anthem when Barbra fades out.

Because of this versatility, CDs cost more than cassette tapes. Looked at another way, the information content of the product is greater and thus adds more value to the consumer's satisfaction. Increasingly, technology is providing products that are higher in information content. These products range from nutrition labeling on food packaging to PCs and software that allow effortless transition from database to word processor to spreadsheet.

Firms are increasingly realizing that they are in the information business, and that the extra value they provide, and the thing that will attract consumers to use their wares, is the information content of their products and services.

Jerry Matthews, the executive vice president of the Florida Association of REALTORS®, describes a hierarchy of information creators, "strainers" and conveyors. Technological change will direct rewards primarily to the creators (those who generate knowledge) and secondarily to the strainers (those who interpret information). Very little, if anything, will go to those who merely transmit existing information.

For real estate professionals, this has a very strong implication. As technology gives consumers increasing access to property information and allows them to prescreen housing options, the value added by the professional changes from being the information provider to being the guide through the maze of facts and figures facing the customer. *In other words, real estate professionals must become information strainers rather than information conveyors.*

$\mathcal{S}$tepping Ahead to Profit$

Examine your business. How much of what you do is concerned with the creation of information? With straining? With conveying? Draw up a six-month program to shift the emphasis of your activity up the information hierarchy.

7. Success Lies in Obtaining More of a Customer's Business, Not More Customers

With the changes in the market leverage held by customers as a result of technology, businesses have had to adjust the way they look at the consumer. William Sherden ("How Market Ownership Works," *Marketing Forum*, February 1995) describes it this way:

> The first and most important characteristic of companies that own their markets is a clear view of the attractive (profitable) customer…. Maximizing value to the customer represents the company's desire to know *better than its competitors* what its customers value most in terms of product and service features, quality and price. (Emphasis added)

Technology has put the consumer in control because it allows the sharing of information. However, it has also allowed firms to change their marketing approach to find out far more about the customer. The example of Publix, which we discussed earlier, illustrates that change. And as more is known, companies can shift from mass marketing to targeted, specific, "one to one" marketing.

With the new approach, the vendor of a product or service measures success in terms of gains in the share of a customer's business, by the lifetime commitment of the consumer to the product and the future value of that business to the firm.

This approach is not particularly new to the real estate business. For years, success has been predicated on the development of a network of contacts who would refer other clients on the basis of exemplary service. But a great deal of this has been accomplished by tapping into what might be called external networks: family, friends, club and church associates, etc. Successful real estate professionals of the future will use technology to identify customers with the greatest lifetime value to them and then learn as much about those customers as they know about themselves. That requires a different mind-set—one that embraces technology and uses it in a savvy, market-driven way.

---

*S*tepping Ahead to Profit$

How would you go about identifying your most valuable clients? How can you know their needs and wants better than any of your competitors? Make a list of your ten best clients. Design a program to capture and store their wants and needs in an easily retrievable manner; record this information. Each week, add another ten to your records.

Future Thoughts

The real estate industry is far from immune to the rapid changes affecting American business in general. These changes, driven by demographics and technological change, are occurring at an increasingly rapid rate.

In the following chapters, we zero in on the specific changes that are going on in the real estate business. This chapter has developed the "background music" against which those particular themes will play.

PART THREE

Changing Trends in Real Estate

CHAPTER 6

Today's King—
The Consumer

"If you build it, they will come," the "Field of Dreams" model made famous by the movie of the same name, was the philosophical assumption that characterized business following World War II. It has worked, often magnificently, for the past four decades. But it won't work in the future, because the new paradigm is "If you *serve my needs*, I will come." *Market success, especially for those in service industries, will come only to those who take the time to learn and serve the needs of their consumers.*

Real estate firms and the professionals who work in them, like many other service industries, have been slow to recognize this shift. Most firms today are still operating much as they did in the 1950s:

- Brokers recruit agents, then give them a desk, a phone and perhaps some training, assuming that turnover is a fact of life. In 1992 (the most recent data available from the National Association of REALTORS®), 13 percent of the sales force left. Although this is less than the nearly one-third annual turnover of earlier years, it is still substantial. As a result, many brokers and sales managers list recruiting as their number one job.

- Most of today's brokers put the needs and wants of their agents before those of the buyers and sellers who pay the commissions.
- Smaller real estate offices are often tucked away in strip shopping centers or downtown side streets, their windows decorated with small black and white photographs of current listings. Larger offices are usually freestanding with impersonal "bullpen" desk arrangements.
- Advertising dollars are largely (66 percent of the 1992 total advertising expense) spent on nontargeted newspaper classified and open house ads.
- Many agents stay in the office waiting for a floor call, a "walk-in" or the phone to ring. Others hire assistants to make cold calls and send out volumes of impersonal mailings, hoping that some small percentage of those contacted will have some interest in selling or buying real estate.
- The most common complaint of consumers, especially sellers, is that "their" agent rarely contacts them.

Given this rather passive, field of dreams approach to the business, it's small wonder that income for real estate licensees is low. Even when figures for just the more experienced practitioners—those with CRB, CRS and GRI designations—are considered, average annual incomes are $33,100 for sales agents and $36,100 for brokers (*Real Estate Agent Profitability 1992*, NAR).

Savvy Consumers Are Rewriting the Rulebook

This "field of dreams" model worked well until the early 1970s, just as it did for IBM's mainframe business and America's automobile manufacturers. Since that time, this method of doing business has become essentially impotent and therefore unprofitable. In retrospect, the reason is clear: "One size fits all" works only until the consumer is presented with choices, which means competition. When that happens, consumers become increasingly sophisticated and assertive; they settle for nothing less than what they want, when and how they want it. The consumer now, and in the future, is in control; *the consumer is king!*

As Steve Murray, coeditor of *REAL Trends,* recently pointed out (*The Real Estate Professional,* January-February 1995), this new assertiveness on behalf of today's real estate buyers and sellers is largely due to three factors:

1. Technology is giving consumers direct access to information about housing markets and values.
2. Affinity groups (people with a common or related interest) are providing consumers with discounts on listing and buying services, mortgage origination costs and closing costs.
3. Buyer agency is giving consumers what they always assumed they had—a trusted agent who represents their interests, an agent in whom they can confide.

Access to each of these is increasing rapidly—so rapidly that those who assume a business-as-usual attitude will find themselves with no business at all.

Effectively, technology is putting consumers on a level playing field with their agents by providing them with market information. Such technology is available today at no additional cost to the consumer (but substantial cost to the sponsoring broker/ agent). Some kinds allow consumers to "surf" the information without interacting with an agent—for example, ERA's kiosks and the Internet's "home pages"; others, such as HomeView's Realty Centers, pair the inquiring consumer with an on-site representative.

Increasing market share by providing discounts to any member of a given affinity group is a common marketing technique. However, only very recently have real estate firms contracted directly with affinity groups. Such arrangements are being made at all levels: nationally, regionally and locally. National franchises have contracted with such organizations as the United States Automobile Association, the AFL/CIO, Wal-Mart and the American Medical Association. In Maryland, several real estate companies have contracted with the Maryland Hospital Association to provide real estate services at a discount to its members anywhere in the state (this is an especially interesting arrangement, as the firms in the population-dense eastern sections are mega-companies, while those in the rural west are relatively small). In many local markets, firms and individuals such as Pittsburgh RE/MAX agent Joe Hirsch have offered group discounts to local employers too small to have their own relocation departments.

These more sophisticated, assertive consumers want relevant information on their terms; they're not willing to read much and they expect to pay no more for *better* service. They are willing, however, to buy both information that allows them to make prudent decisions and human expertise/guidance relative to market value, risk management and negotiation. It is this information combined with advice and advocacy that results in the additional value for which the professional real estate agent is and will be paid.

Unfortunately, according to NAR Executive Vice President Bud Smith, in remarks to the *Great Ideas Conference* (February 1995), only 15–20 percent of the industry uses technology to reformat and package information to make it more valuable. The remainder are, at best, reproducing information that can be found in sources ranging from home magazines to Internet home pages. In the world of the future, there is little or no added value in simply transmitting existing information.

---

*S*tepping Ahead to Profit$

For the next 30 days, track the following for each new buyer and seller:

- How did they learn about you/your firm? What did they know about market values and prices prior to working with you/your firm? How did they get that information?
- What discounts, if any, did they receive from you/your firm, the lender, title insurance company, attorney, etc.? What made them eligible for these discounts?
- Were your/your firm's buyers customers or clients? Were the buyers of your sellers' properties represented by a buyer's agent or were they customers (of a co-op sub-agent or of an in-house selling agent)?
- One year from now, repeat this assignment and compare the results.

Agents Need To Communicate Competence

In this world in which the consumer is in control, professional real estate agents must spend both time and money increasing their competence. To act as adviser and advocate, agents must have a thorough knowledge of all aspects of their real estate specialty, whether residential or commercial, leasing, selling or consulting. Licensees should arm themselves by taking classes, by serving on chamber and REALTOR® organization committees, by networking with others doing similar and related work.

Just having knowledge is, however, not sufficient. It is communication of this knowledge that's critical. Consumers are not mind readers. They know neither how much work an agent does nor how much the agent knows unless there is effective communication. Give new buyers and sellers a full list of the services you'll perform to ensure that their expectations match your intentions (see Figure 6.1 for a sample value package for buyers). Ask buyers and sellers what they expect of you; you can neither meet their expectations nor counsel that they are unreasonable unless you know what they are.

$\mathcal{S}$tepping Ahead to Profit$

Design a value package for seller clients.

In the October 1992 issue of *California Real Estate,* Allan Gantt, broker-owner of Century 21 Accent Realty in Fullerton, California, tells the following tale of two agents to illustrate how not communicating services offered and delivered can be fatal.

Agent Juanita listed a client's home for sale. She priced it right, placed it in the Multiple Listing Service, advertised it in several local newspapers and was planning an open house when the sellers received an excellent offer. The closing happened smoothly four weeks later. Juanita was proud of the service she provided.

FIGURE 6.1 Key Components of a Value Package for Buyer Clients

Information	Risk Management
Properties that meet buyers' wants/needs: access to entire market	Adverse material facts
Description of buying process/documents	Recommendations for lenders, inspectors, lawyers, etc.
CMA when making offer	Verification of value
Schools, shopping, etc.	Oversight of due diligence process
	Maintenance of anonymity
Advice & Advocacy	
Price to offer	**Fiduciary Duties**
Negotiating strategies	Loyalty
Contract terms	Confidentiality
Analysis of future salability	Disclosure
Financial qualifying	Reasonable care
Effect of zoning, etc.	Obedience
	Accounting

Agent Garcia also listed a home. He told his clients exactly what he intended to do and put it in writing. He created a detailed marketing plan and explained the tasks he would perform during the period between contract signing and closing. This home also sold within several weeks. Then, Garcia visited the clients to ask for feedback on his performance, obtain suggestions as to how he might improve his service to future clients, remind the sellers about other real estate services he offers and ask for referrals.

Juanita and Garcia are both outstanding sales agents who got the job done for their clients. Garcia's clients referred

several friends and neighbors to him. Juanita never heard
from her clients again. Little did she know they told their
neighbors her efforts weren't worth the commission they paid.
The difference was communication. Juanita and Garcia both
provided the same services, but she failed to explain those
services to her clients.

Clearly, one can get all the details right and still fail to win
referrals and repeat business, because service must be understood from the standpoint of the consumer. To be effective, the
professional real estate agent must (1) understand the consumer's
wants and needs as well as or better than the consumer and (2)
communicate and demonstrate that those wants and needs are
being met. Good communication results in a consumer who
perceives value.

Price, Value Are Key

There are, however, two basic kinds of consumers, according
to Michael Treacy and Fred Wiersema (*Harvard Business Review*, January-February 1993). The first type defines value within
a matrix of price, convenience and quality. For these consumers, price is most important, making discounted commissions
attractive. The other group is more concerned with obtaining
exactly what they want/need. For them, the specific characteristics of the way service is delivered is far more important than
any reasonable price premium. Consumers in this second group
thus define value by how closely the service offered appears to
be designed just for them.

To be successful then, real estate firms and individual agents
should consider basing their competitive strategies on the model
of differentiation first suggested more than a decade ago by
Harvard professor Michael Porter. Like Treacy and Wiersema,
Porter pointed out that consumers differentiate both products

and services on just two key ingredients, price and value. Both must be dealt with in any effective strategy. One can't compete purely on the basis of cost, and the value must be affordable. There is an obvious limit to how far price (fees) can be cut: When price cutting results in a negative bottom line, a business will fail no matter how much value is provided.

There have been too many examples of pure price competition within the real estate industry. The result has often been business failure. This occurs most frequently in strong "sellers' markets" in which buyer demand exceeds property inventory. For example, during 1994, a highly competitive market in suburban Chicago resulted in companies offering 3.5–4 percent listing fees, with 1 percent going to the listing office and 2.5–3 percent to the selling office. Large firms concentrated on selling their own listings, while smaller firms less likely to sell in-house either stopped taking listings or went out of business. We remember vividly one student who came to us at the end of a morning session to say he was leaving. "Why?" we asked. "Because," he said, "I've come to the conclusion that I simply can't compete, so I'm closing my doors and don't need to know about agency!"

More effective than price cutting is adding value. This is a crucial element of a strategy known as building *clients for life*. Described most delightfully in *Customers for Life/How to Turn That One-Time Buyer into a Lifetime Customer*, by Carl Sewell and Paul B. Brown (1990), this strategy is based on the premise that every client is the source of more than just one transaction. Sewell sells cars—Cadillacs and Hyundais, Lexuses and Chevrolets—in Dallas, but his business methodology is applicable to all business, including real estate, as can be seen from his "Ten Commandments of Customer Service" (Figure 6.2).

The consumer's perception of quality service is an important part of the consumption decision, especially in service industries, like real estate, in which quality is determined by the consumer's internal comparison of an agent's performance with

FIGURE 6.2   The Ten Commandments of Customer Service

The Ten Commandments of Customer Service

1. *Bring 'em back alive.* Ask customers what they want and give it to them again and again.
2. *Systems, not smiles.* Saying please and thank you doesn't ensure you'll do the job right the first time, every time. Only systems guarantee you that.
3. *Underpromise, overdeliver.* Customers expect you to keep your word. Exceed it.
4. *When the customer asks, the answer is always yes.* Period.
5. *Fire your inspectors and consumer relations department.* Every employee who deals with clients must have the authority to handle complaints.
6. *No complaints? Something's wrong.* Encourage your customers to tell you what you're doing wrong.
7. *Measure everything.* Baseball teams do it. Football teams do it. Basketball teams do it. You should, too.
8. *Salaries are unfair.* Pay people like partners.
9. *Your mother was right.* Show people respect. Be polite. It works.
10. *Japanese them.* Learn how the best really do it; make their systems your own. Then improve them.

Warning: *These ten rules aren't worth a damn …* unless you make a profit. You have to make money to stay in business and provide good service.

Reprinted with permission from *Customers for Life: How to Turn That One-Time Buyer into a Lifetime Customer* by Carl Sewell and Paul B. Brown.

expectations. According to J. R. McDaniel and Marc A. Louargand in the Summer 1994 issue of *The Journal of Real Estate Research*, "The key to service quality is to meet or exceed consumer expectations." In a survey of recent Boston-area homebuyers and real estate agents, these researchers found that "buyers want reliability, assurance, empathy, responsiveness and tangibles, in that order." Consumers "are concerned with reliability foremost. Real estate agents should consider how to improve the perception of the quality of their service in this respect. Improvements in the quality of the service product may yield productivity gains or competitive advantage," because "the real estate business is generally viewed as a referral- and repeat-customer business, [and] satisfied customers give referrals and repeat business."

Cultivating a "Learning Relationship" with Clients

Referrals and repeat business are the goal of all agents, including top producer Terri Murphy, who often quotes the lines of a familiar Girl Scout song: "Make new friends but keep the old; one is silver and the other gold." For Terri, as for any other agent, the best source of new business is referrals from satisfied clients. The difference, however, between Terri and many other agents is that she builds on her already positive client relationships through a program of nonthreatening regular (and irregular) contacts. She does this by maintaining a continually updated computer file of personal and business information on every closed client. Terri stresses the personal, clipping any and all newspaper notices about her clients and sending copies of them with notes of congratulation, keeping them informed about their neighborhoods, calling five or six past clients daily just to let them know she's thinking about them and holding an annual party for one and all. She earns her top-producer status by behaving as though her past clients are an invaluable resource—a resource that she legitimately and professionally capitalizes on.

Terri, in technical terms, has created a "learning relationship" with her clients. Learning relationships bind consumers and servicers together: The individual consumer teaches the agent more and more about personal preferences and needs, while the agent continually adapts his/her service to meet the client's complex, individual tastes. This creates an immense competitive advantage that is difficult for other companies and agents to overcome. The company/agent who cultivates learning relationships with clients should be able to retain their business virtually forever, and that easily translates into profit. An individual consumer, over a lifetime, can generate hundreds of thousands of dollars' worth of business. To take greatest advantage of the power of learning relationships, begin with your most valuable clients, designing ways, like Terri, of conducting productive dialogues with them.

$\mathcal{S}$tepping Ahead to Profit$

Using contact software, such as Maximizer for Windows, input information about all clients closed in the past 12 months, all buyers and sellers with whom you're currently working and all closed clients (as far back as your files will take you) who bought or sold properties in excess of your market's median price. Set a reasonable daily contact goal for yourself, then adhere to it faithfully for a minimum of three weeks, by which time you'll have established a very rewarding habit!

Such continually updated, detailed records are a very precious asset that should be jealously guarded by every company and agent. Many companies are beginning to recognize the value of these assets and have developed technology that captures basic information about their agents' buyers and sellers. When agents leave the company, the names of their buyers and sellers are passed on to the new agents who replace them. This, of course, presumes that this information asset is owned by the company rather than the agent.

Other companies, like Windermere, a multiofficed independent real estate company located in Washington, Oregon and British Columbia, understand that such assets are more than just data. Recognizing that the data represents personal relationships developed over time, Windermere terms the data a "book of business" and facilitates its agents' development of their books of business for sale. As a result, Windermere agents now plan ahead of time to leave the business. The first step is to find another agent who's interested in buying the book of business. Windermere helps its agents by working with them to determine a value and to reach an agreement with the interested party. Contracts, drafted by independent counsel, include not only price and payments but activity during the year in which the transition from the selling agent to the buying agent occurs.

Usually, the agents agree that during the first third of the year, the buying agent will be essentially a silent partner who carefully observes the selling agent; during the middle third, the buying agent makes listing presentations with the selling agent, and his/her name is added to the selling agent's signs; during the last third, the selling agent becomes the silent partner and the signs have only the buying agent's name. This careful transition assures that the personal relationship is transferred as well as the data. Clearly, Windermere benefits as well as the agent, because book of business sales usually occur within the company, and buying agents, having spent substantial dollars for the book, are very likely to continue to cultivate it.

Valuing a personal service business like real estate, however, is not an exact science. Figure 6.3 is an example of a business portfolio using numbers based on the current national averages. The commission percentage and splits will obviously vary with both the company and the market. The estimated number of transactions generated by the portfolio is the major variable and depends on the buying agent's capability and willingness to pursue the consumers who make up the portfolio as well as the depth of the selling agent's relationship with those consumers. The purchase value percentage and four- to six-year multiple are only suggestions and certainly would be negotiable items between the selling and the buying agents. The size of the down payment and the payment structure for the remainder also will vary with the agents involved.

FIGURE 6.3 Business Portfolio Example

Average annual income from selling agent's total portfolio	$27,885
Based on a $130,000 average sales price, 6% commission, a 50:50 split co-op and a 50:50 company split, the selling agent's portfolio generates, per transaction	$ 1,950
Number of transactions per year closed by the selling agent	14.3
Estimated number of transactions generated from the portfolio by the buying agent	4.0
Commissions earned by the buying agent from the portfolio at $1,950 per transaction	$ 7,800
First-year portfolio purchase value on a 20% basis	$ 1,560
Total value range of portfolio using a 4- to 6-year multiple	$6,240–$9,360

If the number of transactions generated by the portfolio increases, and the average price of homes increases and/or the listing farm or buyer client base is in the upper price ranges, the value of the portfolio increases. For instance, if the average price is $200,000 and the number of transactions generated from the portfolio increases to eight, the value range of the business portfolio would be $19,200 to $28,800. The value of a high producer's portfolio obviously would be substantially higher. However, all is dependent on the quality of the portfolio and the ability of the buyer to take advantage of this information; there is no substitute for hard work and creativity.

$\mathcal{S}$tepping Ahead to Profit$

Using the form in Figure 6.3, develop a value for your own book of business.

Placing high value on consumer relationships is also good for consumers, as it heightens the probability that they will receive exactly what they want, when, where and how they want it. The consumer relationship becomes one in which doing the right thing for the right reasons results in dependable income for both agent and company.

This is a major change from the past, in which the highest value was placed on commissions. The pursuit of commissions at almost any cost overrode considerations of client loyalty, consumer needs and personal ethics. The new paradigm is *serving* consumers at any cost, even if it means sacrificing the immediate reward of commission. In implementing this new paradigm, the business of real estate is changing from transaction-based brokerage to relationship-based brokerage—a most exciting change, as it leads to long-term business growth. In the future, the emphasis will be on personal relationships rather than just completing a transaction, on long-term relationships rather than short-term gains.

Future Thoughts

The consumer now and in the future is in control, meaning that real estate agents and companies must respond by treating all consumer relationships as the valuable assets they are. The three keys to success are (1) understanding consumer expectations, (2) communicating and meeting/exceeding those expectations, and (3) maintaining contact with the consumer after the initial transaction in ways that emotionally bind the consumer to the company/agent. Creating clients for life is the goal, as only that will result in long-term business growth.

CHAPTER 7

Understanding Shifting Liability

"**B**asically, in the '80s, the brokerage industry gave control of the business to the agents, with the high commissions, use of assistants and personal marketing," stated Bill Jansen, executive vice president of Pacific Union Real Estate Group, San Francisco, in a roundtable discussion of major California brokers reported by *California Real Estate* in its July/August 1994 issue. Jansen couldn't be more correct: A major shift has occurred.

Most of us remember when the broker made *all* the decisions—decisions about commission splits (there might be more than one kind, but fifty-fifty was the highest and agents were happy to receive that); company policy (weekly sales meetings and caravan tours were required, scheduled floor time was mandatory); and advertising (before listings were submitted to the MLS, three quality ads had to be turned in). All contracts, both listing and sales, were reviewed and approved by the broker. Of course, in return, the broker provided everything, paid for everything and was liable for everything.

This paternalistic control by the broker (who usually was also the owner) was reflected in the industry as well. It was the National Association of Real Estate Brokers; the only REALTOR® members were the broker-owners. Sales agents who did belong were REALTOR-ASSOCIATES® who were not allowed to be directors and hold leadership positions. Currently, although there are still a few states that have preserved the REALTOR®/REALTOR-ASSOCIATE® classes, there are no barriers as to who can be elected a director or an officer of NAR.

An Industry in Transition

Today, power has shifted to the agent. Prospective agents are recruited, not unlike athletes. Agents make decisions about and often pay for advertising, write contracts without broker input or review, and attend company meetings and go on tour purely at their option. Most critical of all, agents are paid on sliding scales that may start at a 50:50 split but quickly soar to 80:20, 95:05 and, of course, 100 percent. Before such high commission splits came into being, top producers usually quit to form their own companies. Now they opt to hire personal assistants and set up their own business within the main brokerage. Brokers have become service providers for their sales force, while agents comparison shop for the best services at the lowest prices and highest commission splits and make most of the business decisions.

The Liability Issue

The shift from paternalistic broker to empowered agent, however, is not complete, resulting in power struggles and uneven "playing fields." Remnants of the traditional culture remain, especially in the area of liability. Although most brokers would prefer to shift liability to their agents, states continue to hold brokers liable in spite of "hold harmless" clauses in agents' independent-contractor agreements. Many would agree with former Century 21 international president and CEO Dick Loughlin in his belief that "there is a high degree of vulnerability and liability on the broker in cases where [these] agents are operating almost as separate businesses," a situation that is becoming increasingly common.

Perhaps the best examples of this are the 100 percent companies. The designated broker usually has little or no involvement (and thus little control) in agent activity, and yet the broker is almost always named in any lawsuit filed against an agent. These companies are often large, due in part to the fact that the broker-manager is usually paid on a per-agent basis rather than on transaction volume, and consumers perceive them to have "deep pockets." The large transaction volume generated by the high-producing agents associated with 100 percent firms increases the probability of legal action. Such companies become lightning rods that seem to attract lawsuits.

Besides being liable for agents' acts in spite of having little control, brokers are also finding themselves at the mercy of an increasingly litigious legal environment. Litigation involving agency, environmental hazards and mandatory disclosures has increased legal costs and requires substantially more knowledge and, thus, education.

To counter this uneven playing field, brokers attempt to shift liability, if not to their agents, then to other consumer advisers, such as inspectors and lawyers. Title insurance commitments also become the vehicles for such shifts, usually via disclosures regarding such items as detailed information on special taxing districts and hazardous sites.

Single Licensing: A Trend in the Making

A new trend is developing that could balance this liability equation toward sales agents: *single licensing*. Under this concept, agents would assume more of the liability, as there would be only one kind of real estate license: the broker's license. The sales license would disappear, and all sales agents would be upgraded to broker status via mandatory education within a scheduled time period. Several states have studied this option, as it seems, in large part, to reflect current reality: Salespeople may be responsible for meeting company production standards and adhering to company policy and the Code of Ethics, but they are otherwise on their own in terms of how they achieve their goals.

The major difference between brokers' and sales licenses is that the broker is legally authorized to manage closings. However, in most states closings are managed by title companies, lawyers or escrow companies; the agent, not the broker, attends the closing and is responsible for ensuring that everything is done correctly. Thus, because the difference between the two licensees is largely one of paper, not practice, just one license may make a lot of sense.

Under single licensing, the broker would still have administrative, business-based authority. But, unless the broker could be shown to be involved in purported wrongdoing, liability would rest on the person directly responsible—the agent. This shift from minimal agent liability to unlimited agent liability seems appropriate, given that agents are receiving increasingly more of the company dollar. Such a shift would, of course, require mandatory errors and omissions insurance to protect consumers who would no longer be able to rely on broker "deep pockets."

Is single licensing possible? The Colorado Real Estate Commission has been studying the concept for several years and plans to submit an implementing statute to the 1996 Colorado Legislature. Could this be the beginning of a major change? Assuming that the number of active licensees is substantially reduced (which we'll discuss later in this book) and they become more professional, the concept is a "natural." Well-known author and instructor Julie Garton-Good predicts, "I foresee a broad movement to a type of 100 percent concept whereby agents [operating under their own single license] will group together to fund the ancillary expenses of an office. This should eliminate a high percentage of financially marginal agents from the business, cause agents to require more education [as needed for a broker's license] and definitely make brokerage operations more cost-effective. If the Association of Real Estate License Law Officials would see the merit in endorsing this concept [and/or if several states would go to a single license], I imagine it wouldn't be more than five years before we would see virtually all states headed this way."

$\mathcal{S}$tepping Ahead to Profit$

Contact your state regulatory authority and determine the current percentage of brokers' licenses and sales licenses in your state. Ask if they plan to consider the single license concept. Within your market area, what is the proportion of broker licenses to sales licenses? Within your company? What steps would have to be taken to change from current dual licensing to single licensing? What would be the practical differences in your business if this change did occur? Would you be in favor of or opposed to such a change?

The Designated Agent Concept

A change closely related to but different from single licensing is that of *designated* or *appointed agent*. This concept was originally suggested as Recommendation 2.4 of the October 1993

NAR *Report of the Presidential Advisory Group on the Facilitator/Non-Agency Concept*:

> The legislation should provide for the ability on the part of a broker in an in-company transaction to designate an individual licensee within the broker's company to represent the seller, and to designate another individual within the company to represent the buyer, without creating a dual-agency relationship.

As of August 1995, 21 states (Fla., Ga., Ill., Ind., Iowa, Me., Md., Mass., Mo., Mont., Neb., Nev., N.D., Ohio, Ore., R.I., Tenn., Texas, Utah, Va., Wash.) have adopted or drafted statutes with similar language. In most of these statutes, the broker retains agency liability but the other agents in the office are relieved of liability. Thus, the liability is placed where it can most easily be controlled.

NAR's facilitator report has also been successful at reducing consumer liability. Statutes incorporating Recommendation 2.5, "The legislation should eliminate or modify the consumer's vicarious liability for the acts of the licensee," have, as of August 1995, been adopted or drafted in 18 states (Ala., Fla., Ind., Kan., Mass., Mo., Mont., Neb., Nev., N.Y., N.D., Ohio, R.I., Tenn., Texas, Va., Wash., Wis.).

A New Look at Personal Responsibility

Liability aside, another important (but far more difficult to quantify) shift is the change from blaming others to taking personal responsibility for the outcomes of one's actions. Just as this is characteristic of the mature person, it is also typical of a mature industry; it's another part of "growing up" as a profession. The increasing statutory and regulatory requirements for disclosure of all material facts by agents clearly places the responsibility for disclosure on the licensee working directly with the buyer and/or the seller. Blaming others for nondisclosure thus becomes quite difficult. Some well-informed and respected players, however, like Albert (Buz) J. Mayer III, The Prudential Real Estate Affiliates, Inc.'s vice president for affiliate and organizational development, feel that this shift will be "very slow in coming. The courts and attorneys thrive on the culture of blaming others." That's an interesting and valid viewpoint.

Taking responsibility will certainly be characteristic of the future's empowered agents, just as it is of today's successful agents. A 1994 study by John L. Glascock and Linda B. Glascock of Louisiana State University and George Washington University, respectively, found that successful agents were those who (1) liked their work and worked long hours, (2) were persistent, (3) were learning-oriented and focused on their careers, (4) had a high need for achievement and (5) leveraged a high socioeconomic compatibility with their target (niche) markets. Successful agents, then, are those who take responsibility for their own success and like what they do. This two-year research project analyzed successful agents who worked for large, market-dominant firms—Long & Foster Company, with offices in Virginia, Washington, D.C. and Maryland, and C. J. Brown Company in Baton Rouge—located in two very different markets.

However, current real estate agents are still ranked near the bottom (19th out of 26 in 1994) of the Gallup poll that rates honesty and ethical standards of various professionals. Three reasons are suggested for this low position:

1. Real estate is still too easy to enter.
2. Big commissions make the industry "ripe for wrongdoing."
3. As independent contractors, agents rarely have anyone watching over their shoulders, and the regulators are often overburdened and underfunded.

From a public relations perspective, another problem for the industry is the advertising that portrays agents as "million-dollar producers," giving an image of financial success rather than consumer service. You certainly don't see attorneys or other professionals touting their income; this is another holdover from the days when brokers attempted to motivate agents by stroking their egos.

The professionalism of real estate licensees and firms is, however, improving, as it must in order to survive outside competition from technology and big business. Entrance and retention are made more difficult due to ever-increasing continuing education requirements, the complexity of transactions and operational costs. Most agents truly do have the public's interest at heart, even though the goal of some is to make a transaction work at any cost. To deal with the latter, brokers like Stephen Baird, president and CEO of Baird & Warner, Chicagoland's megabroker, are curtailing practices that "compromise [their] ability to adequately represent buyers" in spite of getting "a lot of flak from agents." Such practices include showing only in-house listings to prospective buyers rather than those from other firms and awarding higher commission splits for selling an in-house listing.

Stepping Ahead to Profit$

Think carefully about the common practices within your business. Make a list of any that might place the interests of the firm and/or agent before the interests of the consumer (buyer or seller). If there are any, are these clearly disclosed to buyers/sellers *before* they make a decision? If not, why not?

The real estate business has changed significantly as power shifts from the paternalistic broker to the empowered agent. However, given the fact that it is the consumer who has the ultimate power over *both* firm and agent, there's still a long way to go. The future, if one agrees with broker/attorney Tom Johnson, director of development for Century 21/Old Richmond Realty (Virginia), is one in which "ultimately, everyone will have a real estate agent much as they have lawyers, doctors, accountants, ministers and insurance agents." In other words, in the future, consumers and agents will develop and maintain relationships for life. To achieve success, then, the focus of both agent and firm, according to Johnson, will be "more on the client and his/her needs and less on the individual transaction"; in other words, relationship based rather than transaction based.

Future Thoughts

Although it's a bit rough around the edges, the change from paternalistic broker to empowered agent has occurred, and turning back to the "good old days" is simply not possible. There are still growing pains associated with this change, especially in the arena of liability, for although power has largely shifted, liability is only beginning to shift. Success in the future will be characterized by professional-level service and the building of long-term relationships with consumers who become clients for life.

CHAPTER 8

Listing Business to Selling Business

Remember the saying "You have to list to last"? This phrase has been drummed into the heads of real estate salespeople. The real estate business has been a listing business for years and years—basically from its inception in the early 1900s. Properties are listed and buyers are generated from the "for sale" inventory. Nothing really happens until a property is put on the market and offered for sale. We still believe that every transaction begins with the listing of a property for sale.

Well, this is changing, and changing dramatically. Let's take a look at the reasons. First of all is the advent of buyer agency, wherein transactions are initiated by buyers who "hire" an agent to work for them. Buyers today are interested in specific properties that may not be listed or readily available. Another change is the increasing sophistication of the buying and selling public. The real estate business is no longer a mystery, and the resources necessary to buy or sell are available from numerous sources outside the real estate industry. Buyers and sellers are

91

getting together without professional help or advice. Why is this happening, and what can real estate professionals do to adapt to this new era?

Marketing Real Estate

A major part of the revolution will be the transformation of the marketing of properties. This transformation is occurring right now with many new technological innovations as well as new players in the real estate business. Just look at some of these names: AT&T, IBM, *Chicago Tribune*.... Do these surprise you? They shouldn't, because these companies have been looking closely at our business for years, just waiting for the opportune time. These are the entities that may well be the new "listers" of properties for sale in the future.

Here's how it will work. A seller wants to sell his home. Instead of calling a REALTOR®, whom he may not even know, he sits down at his friendly and familiar computer, goes online and clicks an icon that indicates "Real Estate Services." From the menu, he selects "Listing Home for Sale." Then he will proceed to answer a series of inquiries, such as address, condition, square footage, loans and encumbrances, inclusions and exclusions, etc. The computer, or rather the electronic listing service, will then search the various databases to determine a suggested listing price and will offer a complete listing service with several different service options to choose from. The listing entity will have the capability to offer various advertising plans and other marketing services, signage, personal assistance and so on. The entire initial listing process will be done via an interactive computer. These services will have a menu of fees attached, including hourly, fixed fees and even percentages.

This process will, of course, require human intervention for such things as advice on appropriate fix-up and preparation for showing, legal advice, negotiating assistance, and services that take videos of the property and install signs and possibly lock-boxes, if needed. There will also be an element of general over-sight of the process, including escrow and title services.

How can so many of the business methods that we have successfully practiced for so long now be challenged as unnec-essary and largely obsolete? The answer to this question lies in understanding what it really takes to satisfy the consumer's needs. After a closer look, we may discover that in the past we wasted a lot of time and resources doing things that are really unneces-sary. There also has been very little consistency in the methods we used to accomplish the same purpose. Yet every broker or licensee has been receiving basically the same type of compen-sation for very different amounts and quality of work. We have also discovered that there are very different types of services and amounts of work required to service the seller versus the buyer.

An In-Depth Look at Seller Needs

Let's take a closer look at the seller. Basically, the seller just wants to sell the property at the best possible price and in the shortest time consistent with the seller's needs. Now, let's look at what must be done to satisfy the seller's needs.

- Determine what the property is worth and at what price it should be listed.
- Determine what, if anything, needs to be done to the prop-erty to attract a buyer and what it will cost.
- Determine a marketing plan for the property that will get the job done most effectively and economically.
- Provide assistance in negotiating the offer and contingen-cies.
- Provide assistance with the closing process.

Setting the price.   Current practices call for the potential listing agent to perform a thorough comparative market analysis (CMA) for the property. This is usually accomplished by accessing some source (usually the MLS) for a printout of comparable sold properties using selected criteria. Then adjustments are applied using information obtained by comparing characteristics of the comparables to similar characteristics of the subject property. This entire process is identical to that of an appraisal, except the agent usually doesn't follow the detailed procedures required of licensed appraisers. However, the results of the final determined value for both brokers and appraisers, if sound judgment is used, are usually very similar. The key is to use objectivity and minimize any emotional involvement.

Can the future's automated system reliably provide this service for the seller? The answer is yes, provided that the new system has software sophisticated enough to be able to extract reliable, objective information from the seller. It will also assume (in order to set a value) that the property meets some acceptable standard of condition, which can be modified after a personal inspection by an outside expert source.

For purposes of calculating the initial offering price, the automated service can access the same type of databases presently used. Information on sold properties can generally be obtained from public records or from databases compiled by the service provider. This database information, along with that provided by the seller through a series of carefully structured inquiries, can produce as accurate a pricing result as that now achieved by licensees. All of this presumes that the seller will be honest and realistic. Issues such as motivation of the seller and condition of the property, as well as some subjective analysis of market conditions and location, are important aspects of setting the price that will require human interaction.

It will be made abundantly clear in this process that if the seller is not credible, the property will not sell and the seller will have wasted time and money, as this new service will likely charge some type of up-front fee. The new service will also probably have some fail-safe procedure that will not allow over-priced, unsalable listings. What a blessing that would be!

Condition and fix-up. Determining the condition of a property can sometimes be a very subjective thing. As previously mentioned, the seller must be realistic; however, it will most likely be necessary for the future listing entity to provide personal intervention for this phase of the listing process. A subcontractor or possibly an employee of the listing entity will have to visit the property to verify condition and suggest necessary fix-up in order to most effectively market the property.

This advice will include specifically what should be done, how much it will cost and who can do it. These advisers will be trained, knowledgeable experts and will help maximize the value for the least investment in fix-up cost. Currently, this phase is usually accomplished by listing agents who possess a varied range of knowledge and experience. There are few, if any, standard or consistently accepted criteria for fix-up work. This can put a seller at substantial risk, depending on the experience of the agent.

The new listing entity will employ or contract with professional decorators, contractors, architects, etc., to provide this service using an objective, standardized approach. They will be able to give accurate estimates on what certain improvements will do for ultimate salability and increased value. This aspect of the service offered by the new listing entity will probably be a separate cost for the seller and possibly a profit center or even a separate specialized business.

Marketing the property. This category offers a wide variety of possible service alternatives, including the following:

* MLS or similar national or international inventory system of exposure

- Company or franchise networking
- Advertising: classified, real estate magazine, special sections, etc.
- Brochures and flyers
- Signage
- Open houses

Almost all of these general categories are used to some extent today, but let's look at how the new listing entity may be able to offer the same or better services in each of these categories. The name of the game is going to be consumer choice. Menus of offered marketing services will be the key. How much marketing does the seller need? What is the market? How salable is the property? What are the costs for each specific type of service or level of service? How much is the seller willing to pay? How much personal involvement does the seller want?

The old way of doing the same thing for every listing will disappear, and each property will have its own personally tailored marketing plan to fit the situation and the seller's needs, desires and pocketbook. Even though marketing plans are nothing new, the traditional practice was for the listing broker to call all the shots. Now the seller will be making the decisions and paying according to the services rendered.

Multiple Listing Service (MLS)—The MLS or similar product inventory system is where the biggest revolution is occurring. The Multiple Listing Service of today will bear little resemblance to the MLS of the future. The new listing entity (which, by the way, could be an existing but transformed MLS entity) will make available to its users the most technologically advanced MLS services imaginable. These systems are available now, and new ones are being developed every day. Such exciting innovations as virtual reality, interactive TV, Internet/World Wide Web and many more are revolutionizing access to the inventory of available real estate.

The ability to input product into this new MLS will be open to all licensees and probably all owners as well. Ideally, the system will contain the complete inventory of all properties on the market virtually all over the world, which will be available to anyone anywhere who has the proper equipment. The system will be accessed through a computer terminal with a modem by going online and using simple, user-friendly procedures to get any information desired. The inventory will be in color and will include comprehensive videos of each property.

This all sounds great, but, one may ask, how much will it cost and who can afford it? This question really has not been answered yet, because the cost to produce and the means of production are as yet unknown. There have been many attempts to do video presentations of properties but never in the quantity necessary to make the new systems effective. All of this will be a major change from the present single picture of a property (many of which are still black and white).

One overriding question remains unanswered: What entity or organization(s) will own, control and provide these new MLS-type services? Will it be one organization, a network of affiliated companies or independent entities serving specific geographic markets? Current MLSs are mostly owned and operated by traditional real estate associations; a few are privately owned. The new listing entity may own or control the MLS operation, or the MLS operation may own or control or even *be* the new listing entity. In any event, the MLS type of marketing service will be available to sellers through either traditional brokers or a computer online service.

Company, franchise or organization networking—Network marketing has always been considered an important asset of the large company or franchise with numerous offices and licensees in market areas across the country. It has also been an important aspect of the real estate organization's services to members. Many listings in a "hot" market were sold "in-house" before they were even available on the open market or in the MLS. However, with all inventory instantly available to everyone, networking will be less effective. Once again, it must be pointed out that who or what controls the inventory will really determine the impact on this aspect of marketing real estate.

Advertising—The entire area of advertising and promotion of available properties is where some of the most revolutionary innovations will be found. All of the advertising media are getting involved in the new coalitions and networks of organizations that are seriously investigating the real estate business. There are newspaper chains, cable TV companies, magazine publishers, direct mail services, hardware and software companies, etc., looking for possible involvement.

Historically, the amount of outside advertising and promotion has been a very unstructured and largely unscientific aspect of marketing properties. Many real estate companies have done institutional advertising and occasionally mixed it with property offerings, but the primary intent has been to attract sellers, not necessarily buyers. Some companies and franchises produce catalogs of listed properties or run regular block classified ads. Frequently, the amount or type of advertising offered to sellers is up to the listing agent or broker and is usually paid for as part of overhead expenses charged against the listing fee. Occasionally, a seller may subsidize special advertising. One thing is certain: There is no standard for advertising, and every broker is his/her own expert on what works best.

The advertising phase of marketing lends itself ideally to the new listing entity, especially if that entity is allied with one or more of the large advertising media. Expect the advertising and promotion package to be tied to a menu of services; sellers will pay for only the advertising they want. The amount and type of advertising will be directly related to specific types of properties and market conditions at a particular time. The future vendors of listing services will have methods and procedures that will make the advertising of properties much more cost-effective, for it will now have to be justified to the consumer.

Brochures or flyers—Property brochures will continue to have some application, but not to the extent they are currently used. Because of the broad availability of the inventory to both the public and all licensees, the necessity for brochures will be reduced substantially. Brochures will still be needed at properties for personal visits during showings or open houses, and there may be some new, creative distribution ideas, such as distributing directly to sources of buyers. However, it is important to remember that the cost of brochures will be an important factor that will have to be justified to the seller. The new listing entity will have resources that can recommend the appropriate use of brochures and cost-effectively produce them if it is justified.

Signage—Signs on properties offered for sale will continue to be an important part of marketing real estate. In spite of the new technological advances that will allow buyers to view properties without personal visits, buyers will still be looking around, and signs will be necessary. The new listing entity either will have the capability of producing and installing signs in-house or will contract for the service with an outside vendor.

Open houses—Just as signs will continue to be needed, so will open houses. However, with the new trends, most of the open houses will probably be handled by the seller directly without any licensee having to be involved. Techniques of handling buyers or their agents will be covered when the seller lists the property. There will also be specific instruction in conducting the open house. Signs will be provided at the same time the For Sale sign is installed. Once again, this service will be one of the options available for sellers and will be paid for accordingly.

Negotiating the offer and contingencies.   It is presumed that most buyers will have their own agent who will prepare offers and handle most of the details of the sale, including the financing. The seller will, however, need assistance, possibly with some legal advice, in assessing the contract and contingencies. The new listing entity will have a staff of licensees and legal advisers available to assist the sellers with these matters on an as-needed basis. The necessity for this assistance will vary according to the sophistication and experience of the seller. The use of this service will be covered in the listing contract and will be part of the menu of services offered to the seller.

Closing the transaction.   The closing will be much the same as it is today. Title companies, escrow services, attorneys, etc., will be utilized according to local custom, and the new listing entity will have assistance available as needed.

Information Through Technology

Some will say such changes won't (can't?) happen. Others know that most of the parts already exist and that they only need to be combined. For example, *Consumer Reports*, long recognized by consumers for its well-researched evaluations of products, has recently (August 1995) announced a new CMA-type service. Call (800) 775-1212, give your credit card number and, for $10, you can buy ten minutes of time to search for sold properties comparable to your own. Where available, the service accesses public records (only 37 states require reporting of sales prices), is very user-friendly and is designed for FSBOs (for sale by owners). The new Windows 95 also offers a CMA-type facility.

Other information besides sales prices is readily available via technology. Personal life histories (credit, medical, criminal, etc.) and those of all properties are available to all with no more effort than a few keystrokes. Geographic information systems (GIS) are nearly free. Virtually every bit of public information (see Figure 8.1) that exists about a location/property can be

FIGURE 8.1 Currently Available GIS Information

Map-able Public Information

- census data of all kinds
- tax assessor data
- crime rates by type in the vicinity
- utility data (location of utility lines, current rates, etc.)
- traffic counts at various hours and on various days of the week
- earthquake faults
- volcanic activity
- flood plains
- topography
- locations of public buildings like schools, restaurants, stores, police stations, hospitals, etc.
- recent real estate sale and listing prices of neighborhood properties
- recent rents in the neighborhood
- real estate property descriptions from assessor's, building permit issuer's, and MLS records
- mass transit lines
- crops
- subsurface minerals
- vegetation
- cellular phone coverage
- toxic contamination

- wild animal species and populations in local fields and streams
- underground storage tanks
- air pollution
- climate
- voting patterns
- title history
- disease incidence
- recent building permits issued
- nearby current construction
- satellite and aerial photos of the neighborhood, including special images like infrared
- videotape of the property and adjacent properties and street scenes
- elected and appointed officials who have jurisdiction over the area
- soils
- building and renovation permit history of the subject property
- building code violation history of the subject property
- languages spoken
- types of properties in the vicinity
- public aspects of neighbors' lives

displayed in full-color graphics on a map. "The result," according to the February 1994 issue of *Real Estate Investor's Monthly*, "is as though every single property in the country were the subject of a continuously updated, full-narrative real estate appraisal."

Geospan Corporation, a Minnesota company (612-559-8000), is videotaping 850,000 miles of streets, which means all the streets in every city of 25,000 or more. The Twin Cities, Los Angeles County and Houston will be complete by the end of 1995; Atlanta, Washington, D.C. and others will be added by 1996; and the entire country will be covered by the end of 1997. Once completed, the videos will be updated annually. The technology that overlays video information on maps (the image of a car drives along the street on the computer screen and allows one to "see" the buildings and land on either side, front and back) was developed by Geospan with Edina Realty as its partner, which means that the process is designed with REALTORS® in mind. Geospan's CD-ROMs can be easily integrated into other GIS data.

Geospan makes use of Global Positioning System (GPS) technology, which relies on 24 satellites that orbit the earth twice daily transmitting signals timed by four hyper-accurate atomic clocks. A GPS receiver calculates where someone/something is by measuring the time it takes for the signals to reach it (this is the basis for car-based navigation computers like TravTek). Integrating such technology with computerized phone book data will allow any property to be easily found simply by inputting the address into the computer.

Marketing is also being invaded by technology. Web sites on the Internet are daily listing more and more properties on a plethora of "home pages." It's estimated that 25–30 million people access the Internet worldwide. A relatively small percentage (10–20 percent) access via one of the five major online systems (Prodigy, CompuServe, America On-Line, GEnie and Delphi);

the vast majority do so through corporately "owned" Web sites (e.g., Du Pont, MIT, Bell Atlantic, IBM, NCR). But however accessed, ads (some with pictures) for real estate can be found on the Internet. A number of companies are beginning to offer such ad space for a fee—for example, HomeBuyer (410-280-8840, ext. 3010) and Rocky Mountain Cyber Mall (303-581-0606). So powerful is this tool that the NAR's REALTOR® Information Network rolled out its own Internet HomeSearch facility late in 1995.

Stepping Ahead to Profit$

Imagine that the date is exactly two years from today. Make a list of specific differences between your listing practice today and that same practice in two years. How would this list change in five years? Ten years?

To achieve a competitive edge in a world of ever-expanding technological alternatives, some companies today are already offering sellers choices beyond the traditional full-service percentage fee. Franchises such as Sellers Choice and Help-U-Sell charge set flat fees that range from less than $1,000 to almost $6,000, depending on the average selling price of homes in the franchise area. The fees, which are generally below the average available within the marketplace, certainly get the attention of some sellers, and those franchisees that are successful do so on the basis of quantity of transactions.

Other companies, like Colorado's small boutique firm, Boulder Real Estate Services, Ltd. (BRS), have begun to offer sellers a menu of services in which the fee charged is directly related to the services elected by the seller. John Harlan (303-442-3335) of BRS has designed a menu with four choices. Two are basically different levels of services for FSBOs; up-front, nonrefundable flat fees are paid for these. Two are more traditional percentage fees. Each choice adds more services onto the basic level. The response of sellers is strongly positive: "This is wonderful; no one ever gave me a choice before."

An In-Depth Look at Buyer Needs

Now let's get a closer look at the buyer. Buyers' needs are substantially different from those of sellers and are not nearly as adaptable to automation. There is also a difference between the first-time buyer and the more experienced buyer. Remember, every seller has had the experience of buying and owning a property; however, the first-time buyer has never been an owner or previous buyer. Every buyer has certain needs that must be satisfied to a greater or lesser degree. The following is a list of most of the buyer's basic needs.

- Community/market information
- Access to the entire market
- Preparation of the offer
- Negotiation for the lowest price and best terms
- Verification of value
- Best financing
- Verification of property condition
- Verification of adequate zoning
- Verification of accessibility
- Survey
- Analysis of future salability
- Management of the closing process

Can the new listing entity satisfy these needs? Let's take a look and see.

Community/market information—The new listing entity may or may not have video presentations on the various market areas. This option is being discussed by several entrepreneurial groups and will be available soon, especially for the relocation side of the business. This information probably wouldn't be necessary for local buyers, although it is important for first-time buyers.

Access to the entire market—The new listing entity would offer access to the entire market to all potential buyers, particularly with the advent of public access to the inventory database and with all listed properties on one system. This new system is also likely to have many properties that are for sale by owners directly and not listed with brokers.

Preparation of an offer—This is something that may be available from the new entity; however, because its primary purpose is to deal with the owner/seller side of the business, buyers will probably be referred to a separate company for representation. This referral company could be affiliated with the new listing entity or may be an independent broker/company.

Negotiation for lowest price and best terms—This service would be handled the same as the situation above and would be reserved for the entity representing the buyer. Once again, the new listing entity could provide brokers or lawyers to handle this activity, but most likely it will just refer the buyer to an independent buyer agent.

Verification of value—Because of the process used to arrive at the listed price in the new system, the values as reflected by this price will be more reliable, and further verification will not be as important as it is today. If a new loan is necessary, an appraisal may be required by the lender, which would satisfy the buyer's need to confirm value. However, even these "appraisals" will be done via technology: Commonwealth Land Title Insurance Company of Philadelphia says its new (fall, 1995)

Statistical Evaluation Report (SER) is able to give quick and precise estimates of residential properties in major metropolitan areas throughout the country. SER reports, which can be produced in half an hour, are designed for fast collateral assessment in home equity lending, servicing loss mitigation and appraisal reviews.

Best financing—This service may or may not be provided by the new entity. Again, it is crucial for the buyer to have objective independent assistance to avoid any conflict of interest. The new entity may have financing affiliates or subsidiaries; however, this function would be best handled by the buyer's agent.

Verification of property condition, adequate zoning, accessibility—Property condition is traditionally verified by means of a third-party inspector hired by the buyer as a condition of the contract. There is a possibility that the new prelisting service provided by the new listing entity will be a substitute for the buyer inspection or at least will provide somewhat objective assistance for this step in the process. The buyer still will need help for this, and the best assurance will be from a good buyer's agent.

Similarly, verification of adequate zoning and accessibility, after an initial computer search for the basic information, will require human interaction with the buyer as well as with the appropriate governmental offices.

Survey—The most important issue here is that the buyer is assured of the exact property he/she is buying. A lender or title company may require a survey that would satisfy this need. Some assistance with minimal verification may be provided by sellers from information they obtained through the listing process of the new listing entity.

Analysis of future salability—This analysis can probably only be provided objectively by the buyer's agent or representative. The subjectivity of this type of analysis is something that the listing entity would most likely avoid.

Management of the closing process—The closing process is fixed by custom and tradition in individual markets. It is performed by lawyers, escrow or closing companies, title companies and brokers themselves. This is another area that the new entity probably will not get involved with, except through another subsidiary or affiliate. The buyer, however, will still need the personal help and assistance best provided by his/her own agent or representative.

As we can see from the above, the buyer needs lots of help and advice. There are a few items that the new listing entity can provide, but by and large the buyer will need reliable personal assistance. One thing is certain: First-time buyers will need their own agent, and the move to increased consumer protection will demand this. Buyer representation (agency) should flourish as the new listing entities begin to emerge, although some of the new entities may decide to take on all of the aspects of full brokerage services, including buyer representation.

Let's look at how the process will work for buyers. With universal access to the inventory, buyers will be able to sit down either at their own computer or at a computer in the office of their agent and call up the online program for real estate for sale or lease. The buyer or agent will be able to access the available inventory for whatever type or price property desired. The system will provide complete videos of all the inventory available, including properties offered by builders and developers. After touring all the prospects by video, buyers will select the one they wish to purchase. An offer will be written, with the assistance of a computer-generated form and, one hopes, an agent; however, buyers will have the capability to do this on their own if they wish.

While the offer is being presented electronically, the buyer will make a loan application and receive loan approval, within minutes, subject to acceptance of the offer and personal inspection of the property. Most lenders for routine residential transactions will not even require an appraisal, as statistics show that appraisals today are generally within 2 percent of sales prices. At the same time, some of the closing details will be attended to (i.e., title policies, etc.). All of this can happen at one session, and depending on the number of properties reviewed, it may take as little as two to three hours.

What about the Real Estate Licensee?

One may ask where this leaves the traditional brokers and companies. There has been a trend for some time now to compete vigorously on the listing side of the business. Many markets have experienced serious pressures to reduce the listing fees charged by full-service companies. This phenomenon stems from just what we've been discussing. The listing and marketing of properties has become more straightforward and routine and therefore less costly in terms of personal time commitment. Companies seem willing to sacrifice some of the listing fee in the hope of attracting the buyer themselves and collecting the selling fee, which has remained fairly constant.

It seems logical that these trends and market pressures would lead brokers to believe that the future of the business lies in concentrating on buyers rather than sellers. Much of this will be evident as the new wave of listing procedures and services emerges and we get a good look at which players are involved and the extent of their involvement.

When considering types of services and the various relationships offered, the desirability of a non-agent (i.e.., facilitator, transaction broker) is sometimes discussed. However, in view of the importance of the "value add" concept in the future, the non-agency alternative likely will not work for a number of reasons. First and most significant is that the typical transaction broker cannot act as the advocate or agent of either buyer or seller consumers. The consumer of the future, as has been depicted, will not only need advocacy and representation but will probably demand it. Another important factor to consider is whether the non-agent will be able to provide full confidentiality, as some jurisdictions, such as New Jersey, do not require the transaction broker to maintain confidentiality. As a result, the spread of non-agency has not been significant, nor is it expected to be in the future.

Competition and market pressures will most likely force many brokers to look for ways to form alliances with the new listing entities by offering services that these new companies are not interested in providing. Whether or not brokers are able to form such alliances, *anyone wishing to stay in the business must create innovative programs and services to attract buyers.*

The Rise of Buyer Agency

The absolute success of buyer agents was assured on July 1, 1993, when the National Association of REALTORS® made subagency (representation of the seller by selling agents from a cooperating office) optional. Because of the perceived liability for the actions of subagents on behalf of both sellers and listing agents, large companies stopped cooperating with subagents, and instead offered compensation and cooperation only to buyer agents and to their own in-company agents. The fact that buyer agents are now generally paid out of the transaction is key to their acceptance by the real estate industry.

Almost simultaneously, several groups began to promote and offer training leading to a buyer agency designation. As of this writing, none of the groups has received the endorsement of the

National Association of REALTORS®, although all have been investigated by NAR education and legal counsel.

During this same time period, a majority of the states, with the strong encouragement of the National Association of REALTORS®, passed comprehensive agency legislation and/or regulation. This legitimized both buyer agency and dual agency, which further solidified the acceptance of buyer agents. Even though dual agency (both buyer and seller represented by agent[s] within the same firm) is legal and a generally accepted practice, a number of states have allowed alternatives, such as designated/appointed agents, in which *only* the licensee working with the buyer/seller has agency duties and all other company agents (except the broker) are relieved of those duties. A few states have passed statutes that permit nonagency relationships (e.g., facilitator, transaction broker).

It should also be mentioned that, although the vast majority of buyer agents are affiliated with companies that both list and sell real estate, a small but vocal group of agents work for companies that represent only buyers and never take seller listings. In early 1995, a group of these agents created the National Association of Exclusive Buyer Agents. One of the primary goals of this new association was to lobby against the passage of legislation/regulation that permitted dual agency.

Effective buyer agents represent their buyer clients through advice and advocacy, assisting them to obtain the lowest price and most acceptable terms. A 1993 study by U.S. Sprint of 232 of its relocating employees found that those who hired a buyer agent paid an average of 91 percent of the home's listed price, while those who used traditional agents (who represented the seller) typically paid about 96 percent. Many corporations relocating their employees and most of the third-party companies (Homequity, etc.) either request or require the use of buyer agents on the well-founded theory that the represented employee/buyer is less likely to overpay, meaning the property, when listed by the employee/seller upon retransfer, is correspondingly less likely to be sold at a loss.

Working as a buyer's agent, however, is far more time-consuming (see Figure 8.2 for a due diligence checklist) than working as a listing agent. Recognizing this, we've found some very professional agents who have personal policies that restrict the number of clients they'll work for during the time period between initial contact and a contract to buy. Should other buyers request their services when their "dance card" is full, these agents simply say that they "won't be available until a week from Tuesday, would you prefer an appointment in the morning or afternoon?" Most buyers, appreciating the commitment and attention they'll receive, are willing to wait. Those who cannot or will not are referred to another agent.

Other buyer agents, like Joe Hirsch (412-833-0900) of RE/MAX C.S.I., REALTORS®, of Pittsburgh, Pennsylvania, have solved the buyer agent's time dilemma by "hiring" assistants. Joe has a team of showing assistants, all agents with offices other than RE/MAX C.S.I. After he's completed the initial, and very thorough, buyer counseling session, he places the buyer with an assistant who specializes in the property type the buyer wants. The assistant keeps Joe informed of his/her progress and, when the property is found, Joe confirms that this is the property the buyer wants to purchase (which often means another showing by Joe), then drafts and negotiates the contract. In return for their help, Joe often pays his assistants a 30 percent referral fee. "I'd rather have 70 percent of five transactions than 100 percent of one!" states Joe. Because of his team, Joe rarely works on weekends or evenings and has substantially increased his income in a depressed market in which many agents are failing.

---

*S*tepping Ahead to Profit$

For the next 30 days, keep a detailed (15-minute blocks of time or less) log of your waking hours. Record what you did and the result, including dollars earned (if any) of your efforts. Code your activity as (a) buyer related, (b) seller related, (c) general promotion, (d) volunteer, (e) family/personal or (f) miscellaneous. At the end of 30 days, calculate the percentage of time spent in each category. Compare this with your results and grade your effectiveness. If you received less than an *A*, set and implement specific goals designed to improve your effectiveness. At the end of the second 30 days, grade yourself again. Continue this process until you can honestly think of yourself as a "grade *A*" agent.

Future Thoughts

The listing aspect of the traditional real estate practice is in a major state of revolution, and the late 1990s will see a dramatic shift from the formerly seller/listing-oriented business to the representation of and emphasis on the buyer. The listing and marketing of real estate will be handled by new listing entities that will offer completely automated consumer services. Because buyers' needs will not be as easily assimilated into the new automated systems as sellers' needs, the most profitable aspect of the business will be focused on buyers rather than sellers.

FIGURE 8.2   Buyer Agent Disclosure and Due Diligence
Checklist

I. Physical and environmental aspects of the property

❏ Secure the seller's property disclosure; give to the client and
get a signed receipt.
❏ Check age of structure.
❏ Check square footage for accuracy.
❏ Check lot lines—get a survey if possible.
❏ Check for flood plain.
❏ Check for possible existing homeowners' warranty (this may
also be a new home builders' warranty).
❏ Check for a burglar alarm (owned or leased).
❏ Check for adequate utilities and types, including electricity,
natural gas, propane, oil, etc.
❏ Check for availability, adequacy, potability and cost of water
and sewer. If the property is not on public water and sewer,
the following should be checked and will require a separate
investigation by a specialist:

- capacity and flow of the well
- adequacy of the pump
- condition of the septic tank and leach field
- possible groundwater contamination

❏ Recommend a professional property inspector whose inspection should include the following:

- obvious signs of leaks, termite infestation, molds and
structural damage
- all appliances as to age, proper functioning and any
warranty
- electrical circuit capacity and proper protection; also
aluminum wiring
- lead-based paint and urea-formaldehyde foam insulation
- underground storage tanks
- roof condition and remaining life
- radon
- insulation amount and rating

Reprinted with permission from Ronald C. Tucker at Laff Stein Campbell and
Tucker.

FIGURE 8.2   Buyer Agent Disclosure and Due Diligence
               Checklist, *continued*

- heating and air-conditioning system for capacity and condition
- all plumbing for leaks and condition

❏ Check for proximity to high-voltage power lines.
❏ Check for proximity to major sources of potential noise pollution and air pollution or other potentially hazardous and/or annoying conditions.
❏ Check for special concerns of clients as to what they feel is important to their well-being. If they are particularly concerned about murders, suicides, ghosts, etc., you may want to check these out.

II. Neighborhood

❏ Schools—Give the client factual data provided by the school district and suggest a meeting with school district representatives.
❏ Crime—Check with local police authority to provide information on crime in the neighborhood.
❏ Future development plans—check with local planning authority.

- Check master plan for development in vacant areas nearby.
- Check for future street expansion or improvements.
- Check for commercial development nearby.

❏   Amenities—check for availability of and access to

- fire station (affects insurance rates)
- grocery store
- schools
- neighborhood pool/tennis courts
- retail shopping center
- entertainment, restaurants, etc.

III. Miscellaneous

❏ Check average utility bills for the last year.
❏ Check real property tax and possible increase.

FIGURE 8.2   Buyer Agent Disclosure and Due Diligence
Checklist, *continued*

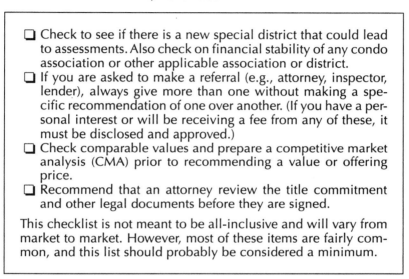

❑ Check to see if there is a new special district that could lead to assessments. Also check on financial stability of any condo association or other applicable association or district.
❑ If you are asked to make a referral (e.g., attorney, inspector, lender), always give more than one without making a specific recommendation of one over another. (If you have a personal interest or will be receiving a fee from any of these, it must be disclosed and approved.)
❑ Check comparable values and prepare a competitive market analysis (CMA) prior to recommending a value or offering price.
❑ Recommend that an attorney review the title commitment and other legal documents before they are signed.

This checklist is not meant to be all-inclusive and will vary from market to market. However, most of these items are fairly common, and this list should probably be considered a minimum.

CHAPTER 9

Restructuring the Real Estate Industry

Darwin R. Reedy, president of Burnet Realty, the United States' fourth largest brokerage, clearly defined the industry's need for restructuring when he stated in an interview with *Real Estate Today* (January-February 1992), "In the 20 years that I've been in the business, I haven't seen a great evolution of services. Brokers haven't kept pace by upgrading their management, agent and staff training, and the variety and caliber of services. Basically, we're selling houses the same way we did in 1965 or 1970."

However, because the way that real estate firms and licensees practice has not been evolving as the world in which the industry operates changes, we are now living through a revolution. "Eradicate [the word] 'change' from your vocabulary. Substitute 'abandonment' or 'revolution' instead," states Tom Peters, well-known management consultant, in his newest book, *The Tom Peters Seminar: Crazy Times Call for Crazy Organizations.* Peter Drucker writes in the *Harvard Business Review*, "Every

117

organization has to prepare for the abandonment of everything it does." Note that Drucker did not say every organization except real estate; he said *every* organization. Why are current times so different from the past? Peters continues, "The world is turning upside down. This upheaval is of the once-every-two-centuries sort, and that's almost impossible for people who have been alive 25, 35, or even 50 or 60 years to imagine. The technology revolution is getting up to speed just in time to coincide with the arrival of the global village."

What does all this mean for real estate? As we enter the new millennium, the sales force will be substantially downsized; firms will be either very large or very small; job functions will be segmented, and many jobs will be automated; practitioners will be specialists rather than generalists; the industry will be a profession; and consumers, as we've discussed in earlier chapters, will have real choices of both services and fees. To accommodate these and many other changes, significant restructuring is both necessary and mandatory. Let's explore some of the early indicators that these changes are, indeed, occurring.

Downsizing of the Sales Force

It is expected that the number of active licensees in the real estate business will decrease substantially by the year 2000. Let's look at why this prediction makes sense.

There are approximately 94.7 million occupied homes in the United States, of which 5 percent or, in 1995, 5 million (the range is 4.6–5.1 million) are sold annually. Market size is thus relatively a constant with fluctuations due to economic conditions. Each of these sale transactions has two "sides"—a listing side and a selling side; potentially, there are two agents involved in each transaction, although one agent may handle both sides.

Commissions have tended to stay in the 6–7 percent range, with each side receiving approximately half, or 3 percent (as we've already seen, however, there is downward pressure on the listing portion). In 1995, the median U.S. sales price was $130,000. Each side therefore has a value of about $3,900 ($130,000 × 3%). This amount is split between the company and the agent (except in 100 percent firms). For ease of calculation, we'll assume a 50 percent in-company split, meaning that the agent, on average, receives $1,950 ($3,900 ÷ 2) per transaction side.

Because most of the active licensees belong to the REALTOR® organization, we'll use the NAR membership as an estimate of the number of active real estate agents. In mid-1995, there were about 700,000 REALTORS®. Given 10 million transaction sides in 1995, this means that, *if* the sides were evenly distributed, each active agent would receive income from 14.3 sides (10 million sides ÷ 700,000 REALTORS®), or $27,885 ($1,950/side × 14.3 sides).

Sides, however, are definitely *not* evenly distributed. In the 1993 *REAL Trends* "Top 250" Report (*THE REAL ESTATE PROFESSIONAL*, July/August 1993), in which the numbers of sides, offices *and* agents (the number of agents per company is no longer listed) were reported, only six of the top 25 companies, ranked by number of transaction sides, had an average agent production in excess of 14.3 sides per agent (eight were below 9.99, ten were between 10 and 14.99, three were between 15 and 19.99, only one was in excess of 20 and three had insufficient data to make the calculation). Of the entire 250 companies, 27 had an average agent production in excess of 20 sides per agent, while 150 companies had an average agent production of less than ten sides per agent. Ten sides is equivalent to $19,500 per year *before* expenses, with no benefits: a low income, if not poverty level. Twenty sides is equivalent to $39,000 per year.

It should be noted that the $27,885 income derived from the average of 14.3 sides per agent is also a gross figure before taxes, with no benefits, and, because most agents are independent contractors, it is also calculated before costs of business, which average $10,000, according to the NAR's 1993 publication, *Real Estate Agent Profitability 1992*. Concurrently, the "barrier to entry" into real estate has increased to about $25,000 given the cost and necessity of computer/communication technology, car, wardrobe, training and education, "desk costs," etc. Such a high barrier essentially eliminates the casual agent who is simply experimenting with a new avocation. Instead, those entering the business are more experienced, better educated and absolutely committed to being successful. Many are replacing jobs lost in corporate America due to downsizing in other industries; they enter with well-honed technology, communication and management skills; they are tough competitors.

As we've already seen, technology is becoming necessary to success and can increase the productivity of agents. A conservative assumption that technology, along with the other factors listed above, will increase average productivity to 20 sides per year per agent would be equivalent to an NAR membership of 500,000 (10 million sides/year ÷ 20 sides/agent); an average productivity of 25 sides per agent would be equivalent to an NAR membership of 400,000 (10 million sides per year ÷ 25 sides per agent).

NAR Membership Expected To Decline

Is the NAR membership decreasing? Yes, according to the annual average NAR membership figures (see Figure 9.1).

Dave Liniger, chairman of RE/MAX International, was quoted in the July 18, 1994, issue of *Real Estate Insider*: "As the cost of remaining in real estate rises, marginal players are already leaving the business at an increasingly rapid rate.... It would certainly not surprise me to see us shrink to 500,000 REALTORS® by the end of this decade. We have far too many people in real estate anyway."

FIGURE 9.1   NAR Membership

Year	Actual	% Change, Year Ago
1988	788,700	
1989	791,000	1.6
1990	794,800	0.5
1991	745,500	-6.2
1992	727,300	-2.4
1993	710,000	-2.4
1994	710,200	0.0
1995	717,500	1.1

$\mathcal{S}$tepping Ahead to Profit$

Carefully review the logic and calculations presented in this section. Where do you disagree? Write out your own assumptions and refigure the calculations. If you are correct, what will that mean to you? To the real estate industry within your market area? Your state? The nation? What effect does the fact that production per agent is not evenly distributed have on your answers? What effect would reduced commission rates have?

FIGURE 9.2   Trends in the Percent of Firms in Various
Size Categories: 1983-1992

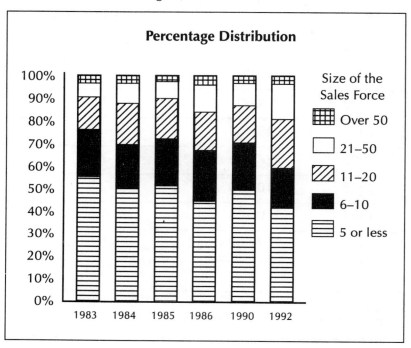

Firms Will Be Very Large or Very Small

Traditionally, real estate companies have ranged in size from the very small to the very large, with every size in between. Offices varied from one-person operations to multiofficed companies with 50+ agents in every office. This has begun to change. The number of very large offices is proliferating, largely due to acquisitions, as is the number of very small "boutique" offices. The small to medium-size companies and offices are disappearing, many having been bought or merged with larger compa-

FIGURE 9.3 Trends in the Percent of Salespeople in Various
Size Categories: 1983–1992

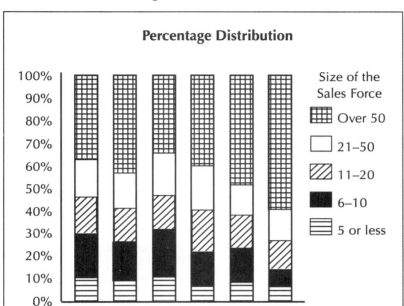

nies, as evidenced by Figures 9.2 and 9.3 (*Profile of Real Estate Firms: 1992*, NAR, 1993). This trend started in the early 1990s and continues to accelerate today.

Consolidation of firms is transforming multiofficed firms into regional market dominators or even multiregional mega-brokerages. Ann Bailey of Management Advisors, Inc. Real Estate Consulting Group stated in the January-February 1995 issue of *California Real Estate,* "This is just the beginning. It used to be that it might take 20 firms to get 50 percent of the marketplace. Now it's not unusual to see three to five firms have 50 to 80 percent in major metropolitan areas." For example, in Minneapolis–St. Paul, Burnet Realty, Inc. and Edina Realty, Inc. account for a 60 percent market share.

Although most mega-brokers are independents (see Figure 9.4), a substantial number are associated with franchises. Overall, franchises are increasing their penetration, as you can see from Figure 9.5, also taken from NAR's 1992 *Profile of Real Estate Firms.* Franchising has become so attractive that several of

FIGURE 9.4   The 250 Largest Brokers in the United States

Rank	Company	Location	#Sides	# Offices
1	Coldwell Banker Residential Brokerage	Mission Viejo, California	104,479	317
2	Weichert, REALTORS®	Morris Plains, New Jersey	56,500	200
3	Long & Foster Real Estate, Inc.	Fairfax, Virginia	46,185	122
4	Burnet Realty, Inc.	Edina, Minnesota	31,188	40
5	Edina Realty, Inc.	Edina, Minnesota	27,814	60
6	Windermere Real Estate	Seattle, Washington	25,343	46
7	The Prudential Florida Realty	Clearwater, Florida	24,919	65
8	Realty Executives	Phoenix, Arizona	21,594	20
9	The Prudential Preferred Properties, Mid-Atlantic	Severna Park, Maryland	21,525	69
10	The Prudential California Realty	Beverly Hills, California	20,356	56

Reprinted with permission from *REAL Trends* and published in full in *REAL Facts: The Real Estate Industry Sourcebook.*

FIGURE 9.5   Franchise Penetration: 1983–1992

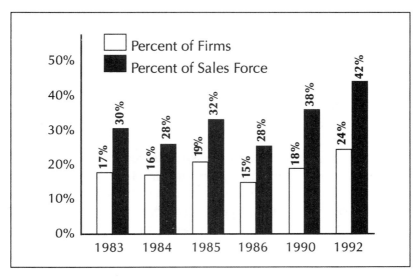

the independent mega-brokers have created fully franchised offices; these include such companies as Windermere Real Estate (Washington), Mason-McDuffie Real Estate (California), Iowa Realty Co., Inc. (Iowa) and John L. Scott Real Estate (Washington). It should be noted that such fully franchised offices are *not* included in the data shown in Figure 9.4.

In combination with the trend toward both large and very small firms is a new organizational concept that is growing rapidly: office/overhead sharing arrangements, as demonstrated by Metro Brokers, Inc. of Colorado. This is an affiliation of independent broker companies (most are single-person entities) that share office space. Thus, such companies can have the costly amenities of traditional large offices while operating independently. Institutional advertising provides identity and credentials similar to larger companies. This concept has grown substantially to over 1,200 broker companies in Colorado and is spreading to other states.

Segmentation and Automation in the Real Estate Office

Job functions within a real estate office are increasingly being segmented into tasks that only licensed sales executives can do and those that can be done by "transaction coordinators" who may or may not be licensed. The sales executives are responsible for interfacing with consumers, which includes negotiating. Transaction coordinators set appointments, do the paperwork and use the computer.

Such segmentation is accomplished in several ways. For example, the large office may have staff in charge of marketing, training, closings, etc. This arrangement has been characteristic of larger offices for many years. Marketing, in particular, is a critical skill that up to now has been left to agents. The future will see this task professionally managed by a sophisticated, well-trained staff.

More contemporary are the top producers—agents with one or more personal assistants, each with a different job function. These assistants tend to be employed in a variety of tasks, ranging from serving as a private receptionist to inputting listing information; developing marketing materials; scheduling clients, appraisers, inspectors; telemarketing; showing property; and dealing with routine paperwork associated with the real estate transaction. Most of these agents have just one assistant; a few have as many as 12. Colorado RE/MAX agents Tony DiCello and Karen Bernardi and California RE/MAX agents Patrick Knapp and Gary Kent are good examples.

These individuals are mega-agents who literally run a mini-business within a larger agency; some even have separate satellite offices adjacent to the main company office. Such agents complete in excess of 100 transactions per year and have businesses with budgets of several hundreds of thousands of dollars. However, the vast majority of top producers are not mega-agents but rather agents who, through excellent time management, use of technology and the services of a personal assistant, have sales volumes in the $5 million to $10 million range or 40 to 80 sides annually (see Figure 9.6).

Thus there is a change from agents who are "lone rangers" to agents who are effectively sales teams with personal assistants. This is an ever-increasing trend, as one would expect, knowing that both agent productivity and profitability increase with the use of assistants (see Figure 9.6, from the NAR's August 1994 *Personal Assistant Survey*).

In this NAR study, top residential brokerage firms as identified by the *REAL Trends* list were compared with all REALTOR® firms (labeled "Designated REALTORS®"); top agents were randomly selected Certified Resident Specialists (CRS) from the Residential Sales Council plus attendees at the 1994 CRS "Salebration." This same study indicates that personal assistants are more commonly allowed by the top residential brokerage firms: 94 percent of these *REAL Trends* firms allow sales agents to employ personal assistants, while just 20 percent of all REALTOR® firms allow assistants. Likewise, the top firms were far more likely to require policies for the use of assistants (72 percent, as compared to 12 percent of all REALTOR® firms).

Brokers have devised many different policies to deal with the potential problems created by personal assistants (see Figure 9.7). Some allow unlicensed assistants and impose specific limits on what duties they can perform, while others require that they be fully licensed to do anything. Brokers concerned with the very real liability issues believe that the role of personal assistants must come under the broker's "umbrella." A good example is Bill Jansen, executive vice president of the Pacific Union Real Estate Group, in San Francisco. In a 1994 interview with *California Real Estate,* Jansen offers the following solution: Have a "three-party agreement between the broker, agent and assistant, which [is] legally a license agreement. It identifies who they're working for—the agent, not us. It also makes it clear that

FIGURE 9.6   1993 Real Estate Productivity (Averages)

	Agent Uses PA		Agent Does Not Use PA	
	No.	Total $ Volume (Millions)	No.	Total $ Volume (Millions)
MLS listings secured by agent	42	$4.3	30	$3.1
Agent listings sold by agent	11	$1.3	9	$0.8
Agent listings sold by another	26	$3.5	14	$1.9
Another's listings sold by agent	16	$2.3	10	$1.4
Listing presentations made in 1993	61		33	

they must abide by our policies and procedures and that I have the right to terminate them if they do anything illegal or unethical. I have some control."

An emerging trend that responds to the liability issue is for the broker to provide a full-time pool of assistants who are available to all agents on an as-needed basis. Each agent who uses any of the pool assistants pays according to the time utilized. In this way, the broker maintains absolute authority and control and is better able to manage the liability risk as well as the physical requirements.

The High Cost of Top Producers

In spite of these issues, there is fierce competition among brokerage companies to attract these top producers, not unlike

FIGURE 9.7   Firm Policy Requirements for Personal Assistants

	Designated REALTORS®	REAL *Trends*
Require license	32%	17%
Abide by office/firm policies and procedures manual	12	15
Assistant cannot perform any activity that requires license	14	12
Agent must meet production levels to get a personal assistant	9	15
Personal assistant is an employee of agent	3	8
Firm pays for desk space and bills agent	7	2
Special personal assistant contract approved by management	9	27
Other	<u>14</u>	<u>4</u>
	100%	100%

the competition for superstar professional athletes. In fact, there are a number of similarities, such as signing bonuses and adjusting operations and policies to accommodate the high producer. The high-volume producer or "empowered agent" comes with a plethora of special needs and idiosyncrasies. These items vary from physical office requirements to individualized commission policies and extra concessions. These demands can be very costly and can also create problems with the other agents. Indeed, there is often a disproportionate allocation of resources that causes some defection by other agents who resent the unequal treatment. Brokers and managers have to exercise careful judgment as to whether all of the adjustments necessary to retain these special people are worth the time, trouble and investment.

Many companies have involved the high producer in the ownership of the organization to ensure retention. Others have variable or sliding commission splits, while many have gone to the 100 percent concept, but most of these arrangements fail to take into consideration the added risk and not so obvious additional costs. The concessions made to accommodate top producers have had a profound effect on the bottom line for many brokers. One of the biggest problems is the inability or just plain unwillingness to make corresponding adjustments for the low producers to offset the higher costs of agents with one or more personal assistants.

Although many top producers still demand high-profile private offices, there is a trend that will be characteristic of the future: sales executives who work out of their home and car while their assistants work out of an office. The major requirement to make this effective is readily obtainable and reasonably inexpensive electronic connectivity. Some brokers, realizing the advantageous economics of having fewer agents in the office, are already offering "home office packages" of hardware, software and other equipment to allow agents to do at home most of what they now do at the company office.

The filling of agents' business needs is thus shifting from a fixed environment (office space, furniture, etc.) to the portable technology arena (computer, modem, fax, cellular phone, personal digital assistant, etc.). This movement toward complete automation is being driven by the large firms that have the necessary resources, knowledge and expertise. The major hindrance to automation is the parallel necessity to train agents to use it. Dennis Moreno, senior vice president of Cornish & Carey, Palo Alto, California, assists his agents by having college students come to the office for a few hours each day to serve as computer consultants and trainers.

The organizational consequences of automation combined with job segmentation increases the importance of the office manager. In the past, office managers have often "risen" from the ranks of top agents who may or may not have had critical management skills. The sheer complexity of business issues faced by the real estate industry both today and in the future requires the development of a core of professional managers. It is expected that these pros will be licensed, but many will not have, or need, experience in the trenches of real estate sales. There will be a tremendous demand for good managers.

Job function segmentation and automation will result in offices that are structured very differently than they are today. Most agents in the future will have "virtual" offices at home or in their car; they will be completely mobile, with the ability to perform all necessary functions from any location. The company office will consist of conference rooms for counseling clients (including use of interactive virtual reality facilities to "show" all available properties in full-color 3D video) plus office areas for personal assistants, transaction coordinators and equipment, administrative offices and some minimal bullpen-type computer/ phone "booths" for agent use. The cost of operation will be less in some respects and more in others, but the very large office with individual agent offices will soon be a thing of the past.

From Generalist to Specialist

As the real estate business developed, most agents listed and sold all types of properties. Real estate was real estate, and a real estate license gave agents the right to sell anything to anybody. Over the years, smart licensees discovered that specializing in a specific geographic area or type of property was more efficient and therefore more profitable. However, the "old-timer" generalist still exists, especially in smaller towns and market areas in which they are expected to handle anything and everything—where, indeed, it is still necessary to handle any type of transaction in order to survive.

Who is this generalist? Many are practitioners who have been in practice for more than 15 or 20 years and are still active; most operate as a one-person shop similar to the general practice lawyer or doctor. Being a generalist, however, can be a curse, because many consumers tend to gravitate to the specialist in this era of perceived expertise and specialized services. With all of the new techniques and technological advances in design, construction and special uses, it is difficult, without some type of specialization, to keep current and maintain the expertise necessary to meet the demands of today's more knowledgeable consumers.

---

*S*tepping Ahead to Profit$

Visit as many companies as possible within your market area. Interview the office manager; tell her you're making a survey to determine the future of real estate and that you'll be pleased to share the results with her. Determine the degree of automation present. Describe the facilities available for agents, assistants, administrators, equipment and consumers. Ask the manager to describe what she thinks the office will look like in five years and ten years. Record the results of your interviews. Review your results: What are your predictions about which companies will be in business in five years? Ten years?

Specialization initially segments the industry into either residential or commercial. Within each of these major categories are a number of very specific specializations. The following is a list of just some of the unique and interesting areas of concentration:

Residential Specialties
- Defined geographic areas or neighborhoods, "farms"
- High-end properties
- Low-priced, subsidized, fix-up properties
- Historic properties
- Exclusive buyer representation
- Farms and ranches
- New development, builder projects, subdivisions
- Condos and townhouses
- Small (up to four units) multifamily properties
- Serving immigrant populations

Commercial Specialties
- Investment properties of all types, investors for all types of properties, exchanges
- Land: speculation, assemblage, development
- Retail: user, owner, development, franchise or chain stores
- Industrial: warehouse, manufacturing, development
- Office buildings: all sizes, sale and leasing, subleasing
- Multifamily: anything over four units up to large projects
- Exclusive tenant representation: all types of properties
- Business brokerage

There are also subspecialties in many of the above categories. Creative agents can make a good living by establishing themselves as experts in a specialized field and building a reputation for getting the job done when it takes special expertise.

Specialization often requires the creation of new types of companies and structures. Databases describing the specialized properties/uses must be built. Contract clauses pertinent to the specialty must be developed. Target marketing must be designed and implemented.

---

*S*tepping Ahead to Profit$

If you perceive yourself to be a generalist, make a list of all the properties you've both listed and sold during the past 12 months. Categorize your list by property type. Are you already a specialist? If so, in what property type—and what did you like about dealing with it? If you're not already a specialist, which of the properties you categorized were of particular interest? Why? Write down what you would have to do to become a specialist in that category of property. Estimate the time required for each item, then prioritize your list and begin to work on it. From now on, keep detailed records of all the properties that fit within your new specialty and add the information to your database, your library of contract clauses and your file of creative marketing concepts.

From Industry to Profession

Historically, the real estate business has been just that: a sales business that marketed and sold or leased properties for owners or landlords. However, over the years this business has changed dramatically from selling a product to representing people and providing a variety of professional services. Simultaneously, the cost for even a single-family house in proportion to personal income has become much greater, thus dramatically increasing the importance of real estate decisions. Consumers began to demand reliable, expert advice and representation in order to minimize their risk and assist in this important decision-making process.

In the early 1980s, courts began to treat licensees as legal agents with full fiduciary duties to both buyer and seller clients. This shift to agency was fairly universal; the courts determined that we were all agents of someone in every real estate transaction. Now, we are considered professionals the same as doctors, lawyers, accountants, architects, etc. Restructuring of real estate as well as these other professions is being driven by three primary forces: (1) increasing costs of operation, which are best offset by higher productivity and efficiency, (2) technological advances and (3) the placing of responsibility and liability where it belongs: with the individual practitioner. If, in fact, real estate is truly a profession, then let's look at the similarities and differences in structure between real estate and other professions.

Medicine. The medical profession is undergoing a major shift to structures such as HMOs and PPOs, which are designed to provide better customer service at lower costs. Most are owned by insurance companies; a few are owned by groups of doctors. There are continuous mergers and acquisitions and fewer small or medium-size organizations. Many individual practitioners have entered into office-sharing arrangements. This type of office sharing has been common among professional medical corporations and some partnership structures for a long time.

Law. Many similarities exist in the legal profession, including a few large national and now international firms. These multioffice firms exist only in large metropolitan areas. In addition, there is extensive office sharing among individual practitioners.

Accounting.   The accounting profession is a good example of the type of restructuring occurring in the professions. It is now the Big Five accounting giants instead of the Big Eight of just a few years ago. The smaller number is, in general, due to mergers. Technology has changed this field much as it is changing real estate, especially in terms of company size and individual practitioners. There is not as much office sharing evident in this profession as in the others, however.

Forms of business organization have had an influence on the structures of the various professions. We see a dramatic shift from the use of the C corporation and partnership to the personal corporation (PC) and now to the limited liability company (LLC). The LLC offers the same liability protection as the corporation but is taxed like a partnership. It basically offers the advantages of both without the disadvantages of either. In states where LLCs are allowed, their use is proliferating rapidly, especially for the professions.

A very significant similarity between the real estate profession and others lies in the administration of and adherence to a professional code of ethics. Real estate's emphasis on ethics is largely due to the strong and influential involvement by the National Association of REALTORS®, which originated the Code in 1913. Over the years, the Code has been expanded and refined to address virtually all aspects of real estate. Its enforcement, while still not as efficient as many would like, is accomplished through a detailed process that seems to work rather well. According to numerous surveys of NAR members, professional standards and Code of Ethics enforcement have been and still are among their top priorities for the organization. The REALTOR® ethics structure is very similar to that of other professions, even though it has not been around as long as some. More important, many of the state statutes that regulate licensees closely reflect the REALTOR® Code of Ethics.

However, the professionalization of the real estate industry is perhaps most strongly indicated by the obvious disappearance of part-time practitioners. Three sets of data reported by the National Association of REALTORS® make this trend apparent; although the time period for each data set is different, the trend is identical. According to NAR's *Profile of Real Estate Firms: 1990*, in 1986 barely 50 percent of real estate brokerages contracted with part-time salespeople; five years earlier, more than 70 percent had part-time salespeople on their rosters. According to the same publication, in 1979 nearly 30 percent of real estate sales associates worked part-time (1–34 hours weekly); a decade later this figure had dropped to less than 19 percent. Finally, from NAR's *Membership Profile 1993: Profile of the Real Estate Broker and Salesperson,* the typical salesperson in 1992 worked a median of 45 hours per week, five hours longer than in 1987.

Consumers Choose Services and Fees

As we've already discussed, the balance of power in the real estate industry has shifted from the broker to the consumer; the consumer is now king. As such, consumers are demanding choices, no longer being satisfied with the "one size fits all" approach to what is usually the most expensive decision in their lives. In this section we'll explore some of today's choices of services and fees, which usually means discounting.

Marv Hoffman, vice president of training at Help-U-Sell, Inc., stated quite correctly in an August 1989 *Real Estate Today* interview:

Consumers have a perception, true or false, that real estate fees are too high, and they want to pay substantially less. But they want the same quality level of service they've been getting. They do not want, nor should they get, so-called discounted services. They need the complete real estate service necessary to market the home effectively and the real estate expertise to see them through to a successful closing.

In addition to Help-U-Sell, there are a number of companies and franchises that have responded to this perceived need.

- Brokers associated with Help-U-Sell (801-553-9999) provide full service and base their fees on the price of a median-priced home and the cost of doing business in a given market area. In 1989, the company's average fee was $2,950.
- Shown By Owner International, Tulsa, Oklahoma (918-272-2550), changes its fees as the market changes based on average days on the market. In a hot sellers' market the fee is as low as 2.5 percent; in a slower buyers' market the fee increases to 4.5 percent.
- Why, U.S.A., Scottsdale, Arizona (602-998-7171), charges a flat fee of $990 plus a cobroker selling fee if it applies.
- Sell Your Own Home of Kansas City, Missouri (913-492-7283) offers several choices: (1) $79 for a how-to manual and For Sale sign plus an optional $29 per week for marketing; (2) $779 up-front for full service; or (3) $2,500 at closing for full service.
- Price Club Realty (602-483-7884 and 602-578-8518) operates out of PriceCostCo membership warehouse stores in Paradise Valley and Tempe, Arizona. Its fee is $445 when the member lists the house and $445 when it closes, for a total fee of $890. Like Why, U.S.A., the seller is also charged for a cobroker fee of about 3 percent if a cobroker is the selling agent. According to Geoff Ward, founder of Price Club Realty, his warehouse-style discount concept solves two major problems: (1) commissioned agents taking large portions of the broker's fee and (2) the very difficult and

expensive delivery, advertising and marketing of real estate services. Given PriceCostCo's 18 million members in 184 locations, Ward plans to expand his company.

With the exception of Sell Your Own Home's option 1, these companies all reduce their costs by allowing the owners to set appointments and show their own homes. Other than this showing aspect, these firms provide traditional full service.

Gregory Hague, owner of Why, U.S.A., in the same 1989 *Real Estate Today* interview, illustrates why the traditional "one fee fits all" is illogical:

> Let's say you have a $100,000 home. You list that home, and you've agreed to pay a 5 percent commission. Whether your home sells in a week or eight months, you pay $5,000. That's silly. Let's take another situation: You have a $100,000 home, and your neighbor has a $300,000 home. Both homes sell in a month, but if you've both agreed to pay a 6 percent commission, you pay $6,000 and he pays $18,000. It's a silly system that doesn't make sense for either the seller or the salesperson.
>
> The sellers list their $100,000 home under the traditional system. The salesperson does everything right for six months and produces two good offers. But the sellers turn them down because they need more money. Should the sellers have to take those offers? No, it's their home; if they don't want to take them, they shouldn't have to. But is it fair that the salesperson did six months' worth of work and ended up with zero? That's the traditional system, and it's going to come to an end.

Most brokers would agree with Hague that the traditional system is not "fair" for either the brokerage company or the seller. However, because they feel locked into a system in which the listings that close pay for all the listings that don't close, as well as for all the time spent working with buyers who don't buy (at least not from that agent), little changes. The size of the problem is enormous: NAR data indicates that there are 1.3–1.6 million listings on the market monthly, and yet the annual sold volume is only 4.6–5.1 million.

The answers are many, but none offers an easy transition. Some real estate companies in the future may charge hourly fees for their services much like the other professions. Others will provide a cafeteria-style menu of services, which is a variation of the flat-fee approach. Still others will credit consumers for work they do against a set fee. Yet others, like Geoff Ward, will compensate for decreased income due to discounted fees by increasing the number of transactions. Regardless of the solution, it is evident from the current downward pressure nationally on listing fees that the traditional system will change. Only those companies that serve the needs of consumers at a price they're willing to pay will survive—and then only if that price is sufficient to pay company/agent overhead plus a reasonable profit.

Future Thoughts

As the revolution unfolds, we can see a major restructuring of the real estate business. With the downsizing of the sales force and a shift from an industry to a profession, we will see a concentration of the very large organizations and more networking of individual practitioners similar to what is happening in other professions.

There will also be a continuing shift to ever more narrow specialization, which will generate more specialized organizational structures. The emergence of the mega-producer with numerous personal assistants calls for new policies and procedures within companies as well as special considerations in the provision of facilities and resources. The increasing automation of real estate procedures will have a significant impact on the practice of both agents and companies, presenting both great opportunities and major structural problems.

Stepping Ahead to Profit$

For the next day/week/month (the longer you do this, the clearer the results will be), keep a log of what you do during all of your working time. Categorize the time by specific transactions and by non-transaction-related activities. Indicate those activities for which you are compensated. How much are you paid for them when calculated on an hourly basis? Assuming that the day/week/month you've tracked is typical, calculate the number of hours you work in a year. Divide this number into the gross/net income you earned last year. What hourly fee would you have to charge to make the same income this year? Because not all your hours worked can be charged to a particular client, adjust this hourly fee to accommodate nonchargeable hours. What is your new hourly fee?

Keep in mind that this revolution of changes will occur mostly in the larger metropolitan areas and in regions with fairly substantial real estate markets. The smaller rural communities will probably not see as many of these changes, because they will not provide the efficiency or cost-effectiveness that they would in the larger markets. The smaller communities will retain the more traditional, more personalized practices.

One thing is certain: The real estate business and its organizational structures, including the professional associations, will be largely unrecognizable within just a few years.

CHAPTER 10

Achieving Profitability

Brokerage profit margins have been declining precipitously for two decades. As reported in the *Real Estate Insider* (January 17, 1994) Larry Romito, senior vice president of residential brokerage, Coldwell Banker, told a seminar group that total production expenses for each sales transaction have increased more than 40 percent in the last 20 years. During the same time period, net earnings before taxes declined from 9 percent to 2 percent—a 78 percent drop!

Pursuing the same subject, NAR's *Realtor News* reported interviews with brokers nationwide in its issue of September 12, 1994. Said Linda Ferguson, broker-owner of Westmark, REALTORS®, Lubbock, Texas: "Most people wouldn't take the kind of legal risks we do for so low a profit." Patricia Green, president of Sun Cove Realty, Inc., of Tampa, Florida, stated, "My firm's been squeezed to half of the profit we were making ten years ago." The story is the same in California, according to Pete Saxon, broker-owner of RE/MAX Gateway Properties: "For years, real estate brokerage was a profitable business. Now, it's becoming a loss leader for real estate brokers' mortgage businesses." In New York City, Clark Halstead, founder of The Halstead Property Company, agreed: "Real estate brokerage is only a marginally profitable business these days, mainly because of the pressure on commission splits."

This chapter will explore the causes of this drop in profitability as well as some solutions for increasing the bottom line. In general, the perspective will be that of brokerage firm ownership rather than of agents, as one of the primary causes of reduced firm profitability is higher commission splits.

Causes of Declining Profitability

To understand real estate brokerage profitability, or the lack thereof, it's necessary first to look at the broader picture. The United States has approximately 65 million homes, of which about 6.5 percent, or 4.2 million, are sold annually (the range is 3.7 to 5 million). Most brokerage income is derived from commission fees that are a percentage of the sales price. Given the highly competitive market, these fees tend to stay in a fairly tight range (approximately 6–7 percent). During the past two decades, sales prices have increased substantially (median price nationally in 1971 was $24,800, while the median in 1991 was $100,391), resulting in increased brokerage revenues. Relative stability combined with increased revenue should be good news for the real estate industry. However, expenses have escalated at an even greater pace and, at the same time, there is a definite trend toward declining commission rates.

According to *Real Estate Brokerage 1991: Income, Expenses and Profits*, NAR's most recent study of this issue, in the time period between its 1987–88 study and the 1990–91 study, gross revenues increased 31 percent while operating expenses grew

35 percent, a 4 percent differential. Most of the growth in expenses during this four-year period, as in many prior years, was due to marked increases in agent commissions (the median commission per revenue unit/transaction side rose 9 percent), employee salaries (up 33 percent) and occupancy (up 17 percent).

Rising Agent Commission Splits

Although commission splits to agents are just now beginning to have a strong negative effect on profitability, the trend began in the late 1970s and early 1980s with the emergence of 100 percent franchises, such as Realty Executives and RE/MAX. The explosion of this 100 percent concept during the 1980s changed forever the relationship between agents and firms. As a result, traditional offices that had been splitting evenly with their agents began to offer very attractive graduated splits while continuing to provide expensive support materials and activities at no additional cost to the agents. In the 1990s, in order to attract and retain top producers, some of these splits were increased to 80–90 percent and cash signing bonuses and "adjustment payments" were given.

The Rocky Mountain Consulting and Training Group of Highlands Ranch, Colorado, surveyed more than 1,200 real estate companies between January 1994 and September 1995. The results of some of their questions are shown in Figure 10.1.

Gerald Warner, president of the Rocky Mountain Group, points out that the failure of 55 percent of companies surveyed to produce a profit was due to these increasingly higher commission splits with no or low desk fees. It is interesting that a large number of the broker respondents (43 percent) felt that their present compensation plan benefited less skilled agents at the expense of top salespeople, and the same percentage simultaneously admitted that they'd lost good agents because of it.

FIGURE 10.1   Survey of Compensation Plans

1. What is your *lowest* agent commission split percentage?
   Under 50%: 6%   50%: 63%   55%: 7%
   60%: 15%   65%: 1%   70%: 8%

2. What is your *highest* agent commission split (with no desk fee)?
   55% or less: 6%   56–69%: 23%   70–79%: 34%
   80% or higher: 37%

3. Do you offer a desk fee/100 percent commission plan?
   Yes: 30%   No: 70%

4. Did your company (as a business) produce a profit last year?
   Yes: 46%   No: 54%

Reprinted with permission from the Rocky Mountain Consulting & Training Group, Inc.

This data is confirmed by NAR's *Real Estate Brokerage 1991* study, which found that 30 percent of the firms surveyed lost money on each transaction, while a mere 17 percent had profitability per revenue unit of more than $400 (see Figure 10.2).

In spite of such dismal numbers, the brokerage community appears slow to react. It seems to be fear resulting from competition that causes such curious behavior. Many brokers are afraid that lowering agents' splits and thus increasing firm profitability will result in loss of even more agents to firms that boast of higher splits. This trend of increasingly higher splits cannot continue.

Increasing Overhead Expense

Rising overhead costs are the second largest contributor to real estate brokerages' shrinking bottom line. As we've seen, higher salaries and occupancy costs are the primary sources.

FIGURE 10.2   Firm Profitability

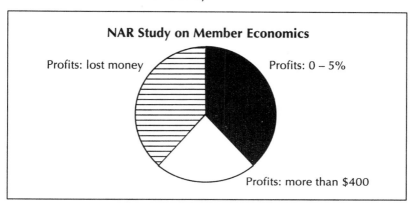

NAR Study on Member Economics

Profits: lost money

Profits: 0 – 5%

Profits: more than $400

However, the cost of technology is also a very important factor. *Fortune*, in its Autumn 1993 Special Report on Information Technology, points out that typical large businesses invest up to 8 percent of their revenues in telecommunications, computer hardware and software, yet productivity barely budges. Technology is needed simply to keep pace with the competition, to survive in the world of information. Just to stay competitive, real estate firms and agents today must have at least the basics of technology: computers, fax, voice mail and cellular telephones.

In addition, there are myriad other causes of productivity's decline: Slow or no economic growth, consumer pressures to reduce fees, regulation, litigation and increased advertising costs are some of the most significant. The effects of the overall economy can be clearly seen in Figure 10.3. Note that 1979–80 and 1990–91 were times of recession. This data was compiled by NAR's research staff in a white paper titled "Real Estate Horizons: A Look Toward the 21st Century" (February 1995).

Although the effect on bottom line is generally sporadic (except for large firms), the business and regulatory climate of the 1990s is increasingly putting pressure on real estate companies and agents to assume financial and legal responsibilities that

FIGURE 10.3   Effect of Economy on Financial Returns

Inflation-Adjusted Measures of Financial Return (Averages)					
	1976–77	1979–80	1984–85	1987–88	1990–91
Net income	$68,000	$42,000	$43,300	$62,500	$32,600
Owners' return	128,200	92,600	72,600	95,900	81,600
Owners' cash flow	153,300	111,700	94,500	117,100	103,700
Percent of Change from Previous Year					
Net income	21%	-30%	2%	44%	-48%
Owners' return	18	-28	-22	32	-15
Owners' cash flow	12	-27	15	24	11

Note: Value adjustments were made using the GDP price deflator.

were unknown to past professionals. The change from *caveat emptor* to agent/firm responsibility to disclose material defects is the best example given that the greatest number of real estate–related lawsuits are based on charges of misrepresentation. The requirements of fair housing, antitrust and agency are other examples of legal concerns rarely thought of prior to the mid-1970s.

Relationships with Other Businesses

Finally, profitability is further eroded by other businesses that want "in on the action." It is very common for brokers, especially larger ones, to be approached by referral organizations, corporate relocation management companies, advance-marketing firms and even employers transferring employees. Each wants a fee for providing its specialized service, its protected pool of sellers and buyers. Most brokers agree, believing that the increased quantity of transactions will make up for the loss on each. As discussed earlier, some brokers are even actively building discount relationships with affinity groups.

Can a real estate office control market share, boast the most sales reps and still go bankrupt? "Sure," said a source familiar with our neighbors in Canada, "we've had three major companies in the greater Toronto area which fit that description go under during the last year [1992]." Such events are, unfortunately, not unknown in American real estate. In both countries, failure can be attributed to not focusing on profitability—on not taking appropriate steps to prevent expenses from exceeding revenues.

Ways To Increase Profitability

Profitability can be increased by two basic methods: (1) increasing revenues/productivity and (2) cutting costs. Both methods will be discussed in detail, but before doing so we'll look at some commonly used techniques that overall have *not* proved successful.

These include attempting to buy a larger share of the listing market by discounting commissions and saturating a market's mass media to attract new service consumers. Both add variable costs that, in the long run, more than offset revenues. Another common strategy that may not provide the desired result is increasing firm size.

Bigger Is Not Always Better

In a study reported in the *Journal of Real Estate Finance and Economics* (June 1993), it was found that "large firms do not command any competitive advantages over smaller firms, at least as far as unit costs are concerned," although "larger firms are still more profitable, in absolute terms [quantity of dollars], than their smaller competitors." The study data indicates that both revenue units and profit per salesperson fall as firm size increases. This is due, in part, to the higher operating costs found in metropolitan areas large enough to support large firms—for example, rent, salaries, regulatory costs of operating in multiple jurisdictions. In fact, larger firms tend to have lower profit margins than smaller ones because of these significantly higher costs (see Figure 10.4).

Increased profitability can, however, be accomplished by either revenue enhancement or cost containment. Which is the most important? On which should the greatest effort be placed? *Revenue!* Revenue is the lifeblood of any firm and therefore should be the main pursuit. There is virtually no limit on how much revenue can be increased with ingenuity and hard work. There is, however, a very real limit on how much costs can be reduced. Some of the techniques that follow focus on increased productivity, others on decreased cost.

Commissions Can Work for Everyone

For most firms, the development of a commission plan that works for both owners and agents is the most critical route to productivity. Such a plan must begin by analyzing the firm's breakeven point (i.e., determining the minimum number of revenue units necessary to cover fixed expenses) and understanding the relationship between fixed expenses (indirect costs that do not vary and that would be incurred even if there were no business activity at all, e.g., rent, utilities, administrative expenses) and variable expenses (direct costs associated with individual units of activity, e.g., commissions, franchise fees, managers' bonuses). Once these numbers are understood, the most effective way for an owner/manager/broker to proceed is to *consider each agent a profit center*. Plans can then be created to

FIGURE 10.4   Brokerage Firm Finances by Size

Median Income, Variable and Fixed Expenses
of Residential Brokerage Firms by Firm Size

	Small	Medium	Large	Very Large
Gross Revenue	$151,300	$542,100	$1,160,600	$4,353,000
Total Variable Expenses	69,400	297,900	709,500	2,662,300
Gross Margin	77,500	225,800	471,000	1,674,200
Total Fixed Expenses	58,000	202,200	428,300	1,633,900

(Percent of Gross Revenue)

Variable Expenses				
Sales Commissions	48%	56%	58%	57%
MLS and Board Fees	*	*	*	*
Franchise and Referral Fees	*	*	*	*
Sales Managers' Bonuses and Overrides	*	*	*	*
Total Variable Expenses	48	58	62	60
Gross Margin				
(Gross Revenue- Variable Expenses)	52	42	38	40

National Association of REALTORS®' 1991 Real Estate Brokerage survey.

make individual agents profitable—which, in turn, results in a profitable company. Only in this way can costs be appropriately allocated.

"Easier said than done" is the response from most brokers, many of whom don't actually know whether they are making money on a particular agent or not. Fortunately, there are at least two software packages to assist brokers in creating a profitable plan.

1. The Rocky Mountain Consulting and Training Group, Inc.'s *Commission Split Formulator* is designed to help the user analyze each salesperson's annual performance, determine the company's annual per-person expenses,

FIGURE 10.4   Brokerage Firm Finances by Size, *continued*

Fixed Expenses				
Advertising	7	6	6	6
Sales Promotion	2	1	1	1
Sales Management Salary	*	*	1	3
Total Salary Expenses	4	7	7	9
Value of Owners' Nonselling Services	*	3	3	2
Communication	3	2	2	2
Occupancy	6	6	5	6
General and Administrative	10	7	6	6
Other	*	*	*	*
Total Fixed Expenses	40	38	37	39
Total Operating Expenses	92	97	98	98
Earnings Before Interest and Taxes (EBIT)	8	3	2	2
Interest Expense	*	*	*	*
Earnings Before Taxes (EBT)	6	2	2	1

* Less than 1 percent

build in a per-person profit expectation and develop a commission split or fee for each agent. This retails for $249 but is available for $169 by calling the company (303-791-8777) and mentioning this book.

2.   Compensation Master's *Commission Planner,* developed by David Cocks of Gallery of Homes/Bowes & Cocks, Peterborough, Ontario, also analyzes agent commission structures and their net impact on company bottom line. However, it includes variable as well as fixed costs, an embedded artificial intelligence that recognizes and corrects math errors and graphical analysis. Designed for non–computer users, it is recommended by the Real Es-

tate Brokerage Managers Council; Certified Real Estate Brokerage Managers (CRBs) can receive a 20 percent discount off the retail price of $895. The software is also available in multiofficed ($1,295), lite (15 or fewer agents) ($495) and recruiting ($395) versions by calling 705-748-6211.

The bottom line for developing profitable compensation plans is paying very close attention to costs, as the highest split must not be implemented until the breakeven point, including profit, is reached. Although some brokers are able to do this with either a hand-held calculator or a basic computer spreadsheet, there are so many variables involved in calculating what it costs to operate a business on a per-person basis that software designed specifically for real estate is highly recommended. For large firms, such software will also make it easier to treat each branch office as a separate profit center with individual compensation plans.

Effective compensation plans allow firms to reduce costs through efficient cost management. However, agent incentives and attitudes must also be considered. There are several methods for addressing this, including flexible commission structures, salaried compensation, paying only for services/materials actually used and attractive benefit packages.

Arbitrary January 1 rollbacks to the lowest commission split are resented by any agent whose production earns a split higher than the lowest. Such rollbacks are disincentives, especially when the higher level is reached late in the year. This can easily be avoided by using 12-month rolling averages in which commission splits are recomputed every month, two months or three months based on the immediate past-12-month average. Rolling averages rather than rollbacks are fairer and result in happier agents, which, according to Thomas Dunn, CRB, president of Longmont, Colorado's Coldwell Banker Preferred Realty, Inc., "helps retention, which helps the bottom line."

Commission versus salary. The vast majority (92 percent) of sales associates today work solely on commission (see Figure 10.5), which should indicate that this is the method of compensation preferred by both agents and owners. A much smaller (3 percent) proportion of firms use salaried compensation; however, they support it enthusiastically because of the results it apparently yields. These methods of compensation are usually associated with different legal/tax status for agents: Most commissioned agents are independent contractors, while all salaried agents are employees. Broker-owners can exercise far greater control over employees than they can over independent contractors.

FIGURE 10.5 Sales Associate Compensation

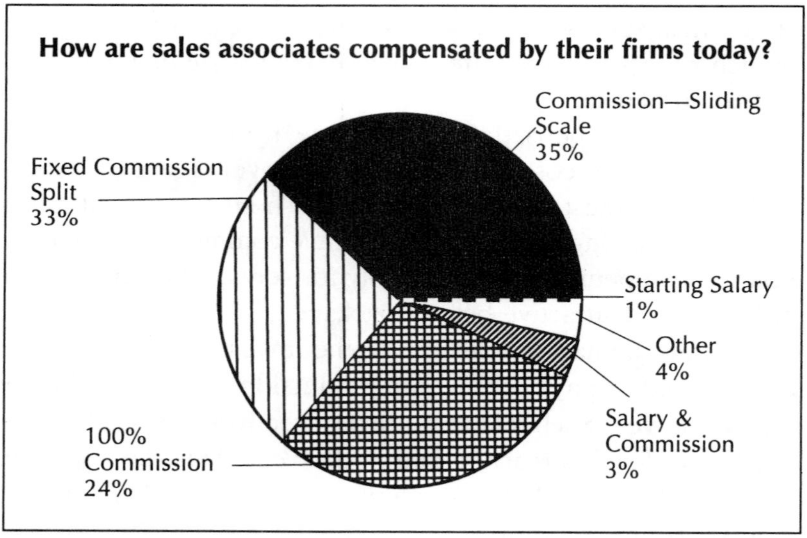

How are sales associates compensated by their firms today?

Commission—Sliding Scale 35%

Fixed Commission Split 33%

Starting Salary 1%

Other 4%

100% Commission 24%

Salary & Commission 3%

Source: *Real Estate Agent Profitability 1992: Compensation and Expenses of Established Salespeople* (National Association of REALTORS®, 1993)

Jack McCafferty, McCafferty & Associates, Spanaway, Washington, has 12 employees, four of whom are licensed, with the remainder providing support. After two years' experience with this plan, McCafferty likes his "control over the activities and results" of his sales associates and thinks salaried compensation is the wave of the future. Australian Neil Jenman agrees, with an interesting viewpoint: "The reason sales associates are paid on commission is because we expect them to fail. The whole system is based on the fact that we expect them not to succeed, so we don't want to invest in them. With a salaried system, we invest in them and they have a much greater chance of success."

Salaries as rewards? Coldwell Banker Professionals, Inc., of Denver, Colorado, reinvented its compensation structure to use salaries as rewards for top producers. Only those who earn a minimum of $50,000 gross commission income can qualify for a salary cap of $48,000 plus generous bonuses. Ninety of the company's 125 agents are on salary; the remainder are on a traditional commission split. According to Coldwell Banker Professional agent William Rottener, "With a salary system, the company invests in you and helps you focus on what's most important—not just getting the deal closed, but providing good customer service." Rottener also feels an emotional boost: "I don't have to worry about not having money coming in. I don't get that sense of desperation that so many sales associates get when they don't have a closing one month. I feel I can better serve the public when I'm not preoccupied with making money." Joe Stavast, broker for the company, believes that significant turnover reduction and building team camaraderie are the two biggest benefits of the salary system.

Ways To Cut Costs

A la Carte Services Provide Choices

Instead of the company paying for everything, the trend is now toward a menu-driven fee-for-service structure. According to Robert Dymont, CEO, Sutton Group, Vancouver, British Columbia, allowing agents to pay only for what they need not only reduces firm expenses but also improves agent productivity. Sutton associates are treated like "adults" by allowing them to "take full responsibility for their lifestyle choices and their own success." Sutton has no elementary training; its offices are large (80 to 90 agents per office), and most associates own their own equipment and do the bulk of their work from home. The typical monthly fee is $250.

Virtual offices. Providing elaborate office space for sales agents whose time is better spent working with clients and customers outside the office is an unnecessary expenditure of much-needed revenue. As a substitute, leading-edge firms are today promoting "virtual" offices, wherein agents work out of their own homes and cars as well as those of their clients via the power of technology. Associates create offices wherever they go by using powerful laptop computers, cellular phones and portable printers/faxes. Desk fees for such agents are kept low by having as many as 50–150 agents in 3,000 to 4,000 square feet. Desks are shared, and offices are used only to meet clients.

As virtual offices are being used by many corporations in addition to real estate, an interesting phenomenon is occurring: the "un–real estating" of corporate America (see the June 4, 1993 *Wall Street Journal* cover article on "Vanishing Offices"). Not only does this change result in reduced time and money spent on commuting, lunches and clothes, it may well have an effect on real estate values, especially in "bedroom" communities inhabited by commuters. According to editors of the June

1993 *Real Estate Investor's Monthly*:

> ...Any neighborhood where a good *commute* is mentioned...
> is an office-related market. For example, Scarsdale home val-
> ues are based in large part on its nearness to Manhattan and
> the fast, comfortable rapid transit connecting the two. Move
> Manhattan's office work away and Scarsdale values fall. Mov-
> ing the work away is what the current technology revolution,
> desk sharing and get-out-of-the-office trends are about.

---

*S*tepping Ahead to Profit$

Check the demographics of your community. How many
people are employed outside of the home? How many commute to another community to work? How many of the commuters are office workers? Brainstorm the effects a reduction in these numbers might have on your community and
the communities to which the residents of your community
commute. If your ideas are correct, how can you change
your business to take advantage of these numbers?

Cutting the deadwood.   Costs can be further reduced by
eliminating marginal agents with high annual desk costs (even
in 1988, they averaged $13,690) who are a drain on profitability.
NAR's *Profile of Real Estate Firms: 1990* defines part time as
working from 1 to 34 hours weekly at a time when the typical
broker works a median of 50 hours a week and the typical
salesperson 45 hours. This survey looks at part-timers both as a
percentage in the industry and as a percentage of firms that
contracted with them; both numbers are declining. In 1979, nearly
30 percent of real estate associates worked part time; in 1989,

the figure had dropped to fewer than 19 percent. In 1981, 70 percent of real estate brokerages had part-time salespeople; five years later, barely 50 percent did.

Retention versus recruitment. Costs can also be cut effectively by keeping a strong focus on retention, especially retention of experienced agents. Just as retaining current and past clients is less expensive for agents than farming for new ones, firms find the cost of retention generally less expensive than recruiting new agents. Bringing on new salespeople entails the cost of training, business setup costs and initial down time while they become accustomed to firm business methodology; additionally, recruiting activities themselves are expensive and take time away from a manager's other activities.

$\mathcal{S}$tepping Ahead to Profit$

Make a list of what your firm does to retain productive agents; be very specific. Make a list of other methods— what your competitors do, what you've read about—to retain productive agents. Estimate the cost of the activities on these lists. Rank the activities in terms of both effectiveness and cost. Rewrite the top five in priority order on another piece of paper and discard the remainder. Beginning with number one, list what you'd have to do to implement this activity; then write a plan to do so.

Exceptional firms increase retention by developing strategic benefit packages for their agents. Windermere, a Seattle, Washington–based firm, recently established a retirement plan for its agents. Under this plan, the company contributes $500 annually for agents with 0–3 years service, $700 for 3–10 years and $1,500 for those with more than a ten-year tenure. Contributions from the agents are automatically taken out of each commission check. Windermere also offers a group health plan. The company understands that today's agent, unlike the traditional agent who entered real estate as a second career, is more likely to be a true, committed professional who needs retirement and health insurance.

Cost sharing.   Firm revenue can also be increased by sharing costs with both agents and the consumer and/or increasing agent productivity. Freelance writer Rick Smith compiled the following by interviewing major California franchises and independents; his report, titled "Making All the Right Moves," was published in *California Real Estate*, January/February 1993.

- Coldwell Banker agents pay an 8 percent franchise fee on each transaction.
- Prudential California Realty charges agents a $400–$900 annual administrative fee; agents are also billed for services and equipment they actually use.
- RE/MAX office fees are 15 percent of gross commissions plus advertising expenses.
- Fred Sands, REALTORS® has a 5 percent promotional fee. In addition, the company has no part-timers.
- The Jon Douglas Company eliminated its 5 percent administrative fee and replaced it with a $250 transaction fee charged to clients. As a multiofficed firm, it has a strategy of first entering high-end markets, then linking those territories, thus creating lucrative interoffice referrals.
- Lyon & Associates has no desk fees as long as agents meet or exceed a monthly minimum production; if production goals are not met, the fee is $800 to $1,400. Additionally, all agents are required to complete two weeks of intensive instruction followed by three months of monitoring/lec-

tures by top agents, then on-the-job coaching for nine months.

- Seville Properties pays for assistants, assuming all legal and financial risks associated with their use; agents can use the services of the assistants by paying a fee of $15 per month.

Coldwell Banker's Larry Romito offers these additional ideas to reduce costs:

- Renegotiate existing occupancy leases, especially if your office is in an area where vacancies are high.
- Use Board of REALTOR® and industry training instead of developing customized programs of your own.
- Tie personnel levels and pay to production output.
- Manage expenses so that they follow rather than lead revenue. Measure income on business opens as well as closes and be ready to adjust expenses accordingly.
- Work with the Board of REALTORS® to shift the burden of board fees collection from the brokerage office to the board.
- Reduce high-cost, low-yield promotional programs, such as classified advertising.
- Increase desk sharing among unproductive agents.
- Establish a profit-sharing bonus for expense reductions and include agents as well as support personnel.
- Eliminate sales associates' receivables and establish a pay-as-you-go system.
- Reduce overhead personnel to 75 percent of what you think you need and make them grow.

As NAR's 1994 edition of *Real Estate Horizons* states, "Increasing agent productivity is the most obvious method available to combat rising costs and to increase profitability." The most effective and efficient way to achieve this is to combine experienced agents with both adequate technological resources and ongoing, real estate–specific training. On average, five to seven years of experience are required before agents reach their optimum earning potential. This is because "On-the-job training is ... the most important element of a salesperson's education. It is only through repetition that a salesperson develops the knowledge and skill required to establish a successful pattern of listing and selling a home." (NAR's *Real Estate Agent Profitability: 1992*)

Professionalizing the Practice of Real Estate

As we've seen, the industry is, indeed, in transition, from consisting of a large number of new agents to a smaller group of more senior professional consultants. These individuals can add value to a transaction by using technology to translate real estate information into meaningful real estate knowledge for the consumer. They also use technology to increase income by expanding the number of people they contact and by downloading MLS information into personal, portable computers, thus creating portable offices. Computers literally become personal assistants that inhabit virtual offices. These pros are top producers who yield increased unit sales and higher profit with fewer people.

Diversification into Ancillary Services

Many firms, large and small, attempt to remain profitable via diversification, providing not only brokerage but related services to their buyer and seller consumers. This one-stop-shopping concept results in real estate companies that also may offer title insurance, homebuilding, escrow, home inspections, home warranties, decorating, training, computer service bureaus, property management, relocation management, real estate schools, mortgage banking, mortgage brokerage, financial management and homeowners insurance, along with other services.

With the recent changes in the RESPA statute, computerized loan origination is becoming a very important ancillary service for many firms. Given the support of technology, firms can take a loan application as soon as a relationship with the buyer is established. Buyers working with such firms can have a competitive edge if a firm loan approval is attached to their purchase offers. In mid-1995, nine of the Masterminds (a national group of large independent firms) announced availability of the first interactive system. CD-ROM based, the system has been developed with Intel and will result in 24-hour loan approvals (contingent on appraisal).

Such diversification is the way of the future. It is, however, not without cost, and in this world of required disclosure there is no guarantee that the consumer will be satisfied to buy such services "in-house." Other firms have not only diversified but, like Prudential California Realty in Beverly Hills, have become aggressive in acquiring competing companies, especially during periods of market slowdown.

Focus on in-house sales.   Greater profitability can also result from focusing on selling company listings rather than those listed by other brokers. Firms that sell a higher portion of in-house sales keep a larger portion of the gross revenue. NAR statistics *(Real Estate Brokerage 1991)* show that in comparison with low (less than 50 percent) and medium (50–74 percent) in-house sales firms, the high (75+ percent) in-house sales firms tend to be smaller, serving smaller, less urban markets. Profitability (earnings before taxes) of these high in-house sales companies is significantly higher (18 percent of gross revenue) than that of low (7 percent) and medium (4 percent) in-house sales firms (see Figure 10.6).

Affinity-based relationships.   As mentioned in Chapter 6, forming discount relationships with affinity groups (employers, associations, unions, etc.) is becoming an increasingly large

FIGURE 10.6   Effect on In-House Sales

Average Income, Variable and Fixed Expenses of Residential Brokerage Firms by In-House Sales

	Low	Medium	High
Gross Revenue	$1,625,200	$1,956,400	$1,111,300
Total Variable Expenses	975,200	1,179,400	602,100
Gross Margin	650,000	777,000	509,200
Total Fixed Expenses	609,500	726,000	428,800

(Percent of Gross Revenue)

	Low	Medium	High
Variable Expenses			
Total Sales Commissions	52%	51%	39%
MLS and Board Fees	*	*	1
Franchise and Referral Fees	1	2	1
Sales Managers' Bonuses and Overrides	1	1	*
Total Variable Expenses	52	53	40
Gross Margin			
(Gross Revenue - Variable Expenses)	48	47	47
Fixed Expenses			
Total Advertising Expenses	7	8	8
Total Sales Promotion Expenses	2	2	2
Sales Managers' Salary	1	2	1
Total Salary Expenses	7	8	5
Value of Owners' Nonselling Services	4	4	3
Total Communication Expenses	2	3	3
Total Occupancy Expenses	7	7	7
Total General and Administrative Expenses	9	8	12
Total of Other Expenses	1	1	1
Total Fixed Expenses	40	42	41
Total Operating Expenses	93	95	81
Earnings Before Interest and Taxes (EBIT)	7	5	19
Interest Expense	1	1	1
Earnings Before Taxes (EBT)	7	4	18

* Less than 1 percent.

source of business for national, regional and local real estate players of all sizes. Steve Murray, co-editor of *REAL Trends*, predicts that the volume of affinity-based transactions will dwarf the corporate relocation market. As Murray says, "Affinity group purchasers are here to stay. The door was opened 30 years ago with the formation of the first referral network." In today's market, "the customer who is not yours is someone else's; there will always be someone trying to improve on your offering."

An interesting example of this is an offering by New West Financial Services, Westlake Village, California. Haven Burke, president of the company, has created a referral network in which buyers and sellers refer themselves. If a relocating family sells a home, the listing and cooperating brokers receive a commission, and the family receives a portion of the referred broker's commission. If people refer themselves to the system as sellers *and* buyers, they receive rebates from *both* the listing and cooperating brokers' commissions. The network does not accept referrals from brokers; it only deals directly with consumers. As of 1993, according to Burke, the program was available in about 40 states. Because state regulations vary, New West checks with each state's real estate commission to confirm that it approves the process.

The Colorado Real Estate Commission has taken Burke's concept one step further in what may be the way of the future. According to a 1995 position of the commission, referral fees may be paid to unlicensed persons so long as the referrer does not engage in any activity for which a real estate license is required, but merely gives a broker the name of a prospective buyer or seller.

Increased market share, however, is best obtained by developing value-based services that are both profitable and competitive in nature. Examples are generally based on consumer fears and unfilled needs. Shannon & Luchs, a Washington, D.C. mega-broker, has instituted a free program that offers to pay the home mortgage payment (up to $1,500 for a maximum of six months) for any of its customers who lose their jobs due to economic conditions or are laid off by their employers. Two other mega-brokers, Prudential Florida Realty and Coldwell Banker Chicago, have harnessed the bilingual ability of some of their agents. Prudential Florida offers foreign-language contracts and designates those agents who speak a second language (about 20 percent) and take special training as International Marketing Specialists. Coldwell Banker Chicago has identified agents with fluency in 46 different languages and compiled a flyer, "We Speak Your Language," that lists the agent's name, language, phone and office location.

---

*S*tepping Ahead to Profit$

The causes of decreased profitability and their remedies form a complex web of relationships between the basic profit equation and the rapidly evolving opportunities for competitive performance. Review the chart in Figure 10.7 and formulate your own "get well plan" by (1) identifying the top three causes of your decreased profits; (2) identifying the three remedies you feel will be most effective; (3) making a detailed list of what must be done to implement those remedies; and (4) developing a time line to put these implementation steps in motion.

Although maintaining a profitable firm requires detailed and creative planning, monitoring and continual readjustment, it just may be that time is also on the side of the real estate industry. According to a recent Cornell University study coauthored by Professor Michael Rendall, the nation's 77 million baby boomers,

FIGURE 10.7   Planning for Profitability

Solution Techniques/Remedies

Causes of Declining Profitability	Higher Value Services	Technology/ Virtual Offices	Compensation Plans	Benefit Plans	Selective Retention	Cost/Expense Management	Other: ___
Low Agent Productivity							
High Agent Splits							
High Employee Salaries							
High Occupancy Costs							
High Variable Costs							
Cost of Technology							
Low Commissions							
Other: ___							

Causes of Declining Profitability

who currently range in age from 30 to almost 50, are going to inherit more than $10 trillion from their parents over the next several decades. Rendall estimates that there will be 115 million bequests averaging $90,000 each. Other studies of boomers—for example, a 1993 study conducted for the Equitable Life Assurance Society—found that 65 percent of this large generation (which used to be called the "me" generation) is placing a new emphasis on savings. (In the past, a real lack of a savings mentality created a major hurdle for first-time homebuyers.) This increased fiscal responsibility is beginning to result in a sizable proportion of this inheritance being invested in real estate.

Future Thoughts

Real estate firm profitability has been declining significantly over the past two decades. Although there are multiple causes, much of this decline can be attributed to increasingly higher commission splits.

Returning firms to profitability requires two basic steps: revenue enhancement and expense reduction. There are many ways to accomplish these goals, but each firm must create its own solution—a process that requires both creativity and teamwork between broker-owners and today's empowered agents.

PART FOUR

Winning Through Reinvention

CHAPTER 11

Your Keys to Future Success

An old friend, comic strip character Pogo, once said, "We are confronted with insurmountable opportunities." This is truly the case in today's world of accelerating change, which frustrates our plans for the future and forces us to prepare for the unexpected. Without a clear vision of the future five to ten years out, the techniques of strategic planning are ineffective. Instead, we must combine skillful short-term planning with flexible response capabilities driven by computer-assisted monitoring of potential scenarios (termed scenario planning by some). In other words, change ain't pretty, nor is it easy!

To achieve success in such an environment requires the ability to make decisions based not on the available but insufficient information, but rather on intuitive judgment. Those who achieve the competitive edge will have faith and trust in their own judgment and the courage to leave the familiar and move into the new unknown.

This may seem like a tall order if you've never seen yourself as a pioneer, if creativity is not one of your strong points. There are, however, important skills that can be learned that will make you, if not comfortable with the future, at least effective in dealing with this environment of constant and accelerating change. These skills are *excellence, innovation* and *anticipation.*

To effectively deal with the future, all three skills are necessary. Having less than all three is like having just one or two legs on a three-legged stool: The stool will simply not stand up. Likewise, a firm or agent with only one or two of these skills will not succeed in the revolutionary new future. A firm/agent known for excellent skills and service but without innovation and anticipation will lose business and become a historical footnote. The innovators who lack excellence and anticipation will create ineffective products or services and find themselves on the bleeding edge rather than the leading edge. Those who anticipate well but don't have the skills of excellence and innovation are the soothsayers unable to implement an effective response to an expected future.

We'll look at these three skills one by one. For each, we'll offer examples and methods of implementation. As we determined earlier, the focus of these three skills must be on product leadership, operational excellence and client intimacy. Learning them requires commitment and a great deal of self-direction, as there is very little training available, although there are excellent books and articles (see the bibliography in the appendix). The rewards, however, both personally and businesswise, will be great, making the time and effort necessary well worthwhile.

Excellence

Paraphrasing Joel A. Barker (*Paradigms: The Business of Discovering the Future,* 1993), excellence has been a competitive edge; however, by the turn of the century it will be the *neces-*

sary price of entry for any business, including real estate. Excellence and quality are essentially synonymous; however, quality is perceived to have gradations, while excellence is simply the best. Excellence is fluid, a process rather than a destination; it requires constant pursuit and an attitude that seeks continuous improvement at all levels of any business. The Japanese first introduced this concept into business and industry. Their word, *kaizen*, means the ability to make very small improvements in processes, products and services *every* day.

Because excellence requires a process of continuous improvement, it is never a goal to be achieved—for as soon as it's achieved, someone will find a way of doing it better, whatever "it" may be. The pursuit of excellence is therefore a long-term commitment and must drive every business activity. It must be consistently emphasized and expected. Excellence must come first.

TQM for the Real Estate Industry

The most common methodology for instilling such attitudes into an organization is Total Quality Management (TQM). Gary Allhiser of Great Visions Consulting (P.O. Box 17288, Fountain Hills, AZ 85296, 602-837-0830), a frequent consultant for real estate associations and companies, has adapted TQM's key principles for the real estate industry (see Figure 11.1).

Because excellence results from a belief that everything can be done better, from an attitude that quality is primary and from a value that places the consumer's needs above all else, it should be clear that once quality has been compromised, few organizations can ever achieve excellence. The pursuit of excellence is not something that one does occasionally or only when one has time; it is a pursuit that must permeate the lifetime of both individual agent and entire firm.

How does excellence play out within real estate, which is a service industry? *We don't sell real estate; owners of real estate*

FIGURE 11.1   TQM Key Principles

Key Principles of Total Quality Management (TQM) for REALTORS®

1. *Quality must come first.* Each REALTOR® needs to develop a set of TQM principles that reflects his/her own needs. The same can be said of any independent agency or franchise. In most organizations, everyone must commit to TQM or it cannot work. An advantage enjoyed in real estate is that, while full participation through an agency is highly desirable, the independent nature of the profession makes it possible for an individual REALTOR® to adopt TQM on his/her own.

2. *Owner-brokers and their associates must not get trapped in "VNOs."* Visible Numbers Only (VNOs) are the principal trap that American management has fallen into. Visible numbers are the short-term profits and input and output measures that business schools have so overemphasized during the last two decades. While simple measures such as profit, numbers of properties listed or sold and the like are useful and informative, they must not become the definitive measures of performance. The only definitive measure of performance should be the extent to which the REALTOR® is conforming to the requirements of his/her customers.

3. *Every person in the agency has a customer and must know who that customer is.* TQM is customer-driven. A customer is someone who benefits from a product or service an individual offers. In real estate the ultimate customer is usually the buyer or seller, depending upon the contract. However, there are many other critical primary customer relationships: The owner-broker has a customer relationship with his/her associates; there is a customer relationship with the lenders and the title companies; there are customer relationships among REALTORS® and their professional associations. Often these various customers have unarticulated and even conflicting requirements that must be identified and resolved if quality service truly is to be offered. Ultimately, viable *partnerships* between and among these different customer groups must be created, maintained and nurtured.

FIGURE 11.1   TQM Key Principles, *continued*

---

4. *Quality is not an end result to be achieved; it is a process of continuous improvement.* Continuous improvement is the life-blood of an organization. Any product or service can be improved. Real estate firms must evolve and continuously improve ahead of their clients' needs if they are to be thought of as the "preferred provider of real estate services" in their communities.

5. *Quality is a long-term commitment.* This teaching causes most American companies to lose interest in TQM. If the REALTOR® is focused upon short-term sales, listings or some other VNO, the pressures to drop TQM in favor of some new quick fix are likely to be insurmountable. Massive owner-broker and agent reeducation, along with a fundamental change in business philosophy, are long-term efforts. A REALTOR® must recognize that the minimum commitment in terms of realizing significant and sustainable dollar savings and income growth is at least five years.

---

*sell their properties. The only thing either agent or firm has to sell is **quality service** and **quality information**; if the service and information are not excellent, there is little or no value added to the transaction.* Recent survey results reported by Gene H. Cheatham, CAE, president of The Murphy Group (407-282-5596), indicate that not only is much of today's service not excellent but that the effect, as might be expected, is a serious loss of business (see Figure 11.2).

A 25 percent dissatisfaction rate is simply *not* acceptable, especially when the transaction is one of the most significant in the lives of both buyers and sellers. In the past, the real estate industry was able to survive such poor performance because the consumer had no choice. But as we have learned, the consumer now has options and is therefore in charge: The REALTOR® is no longer "the only game in town."

FIGURE 11.2 Results of Dissatisfaction

1. One in four clients/customers are angry enough with their agent's service to not do business with them again, but only 4 percent of these will ever complain.

2. Satisfied clients/customers on average tell eight others, whereas the dissatisfied will tell 20.

3. Ninety percent of the dissatisfied will never return, but 70 percent of these will if their problems are solved.

4. It's five times more expensive to get a new customer/client than to keep an old one.

For example, in 1995 Microsoft began beta testing software that provides consumers easy access to comparative market analyses as well as to what's listed and sold. The ability to do this without access to the MLS is due to technology: The current nine-digit ZIP code can identify up to 999,999,999 parcels. According to the American Home Survey, there are only 94.7 million occupied homes in the United States, which means that each of these (as well as all nonresidential properties) can have a unique numerical identification. Combining this with current GIS (Geographic Information Systems, a property mapping software) and assessor's information in one huge database that can be updated instantly as changes occur makes Microsoft's product both possible and practical. *Coincidentally, the National Association of REALTORS®' REALTOR® Information Network (RIN) will provide a similar service, with integration into all of the REALTOR®-owned MLSs; RIN was also being beta tested in 1995.*

Consumers, of course, want more than just information, and they certainly need more information than just what Microsoft or newspapers or any other vendor can provide. When asked about what they wanted in a transaction, consumers listed information as one of eight dominant preferences. The others were speed, convenience, choice, value added, discounts, quality and service. These other seven, all of which have been discussed in earlier chapters, bring us right back to the skills we've identified as being necessary to deal with the future, especially those of excellence and innovation.

---

*S*tepping Ahead to Profit$

From your list of past clients, invite (randomly) five to nine to participate in a focus group. The goal is to determine the level of quality of your service and what you can do to improve it. Ask questions like these: (1) If you had the transaction to do over again, what would you like to see done differently? (2) What could we have done that we didn't do? (3) What did we do really well? (4) What could we have done better?

Based on the responses, prepare a business plan for changes that will increase the perception of excellence. At least every quarter, repeat this assignment with one or more focus groups.

Innovation

According to Joel Barker, several critical and very beneficial effects have been observed among those who make the commitment to excellence: (1) increased innovation, (2) self-management, (3) a return to artistry and craftsmanship and (4) a return of spirit to the workplace. Of these, it is innovation, however, that is the key to attaining a competitive edge.

In a world in which technology allows consumers to do parts of the transaction for themselves, the innovative services and products must *add value* to the real estate transaction. The innovations must make the transaction faster or smoother and/or they must assist consumers in sorting through mountains of information for just those pieces that will allow them to make timely decisions, and/or they must protect consumers from liability and the unknown.

Innovation can be many different things—a new way of providing an old service, an alternative explanation, a change in perspective that revolutionizes the way business is done, a new methodology, a new insight. By definition, it is the process of making changes.

Innovation, however, whether it be buyer agency instead of subagency or a menu of services for sellers instead of a single commission rate, usually challenges existing paradigms and certainly existing practices. As a result, innovation may cause emotional reactions and even complaints from competitors (see Figure 11.3), an effect the innovator should expect. When such reactions do occur, listen to them, then follow with a simple "thank you" and/or quietly provide information to counter objections.

Making the Leap of Faith

To be an innovator, to get ahead of the waves of change we've described at the beginning of this book, it's almost always necessary to trust your intuition and use nonrational judgment—in other words, make a leap of faith. You'll simply never have enough proof to make a truly rational judgment. These changes are self-directed rather than imposed by the environment. They are changes that innovators begin before the current wave of change reaches its crest—changes that are made on the basis of intuition and suspicions, and without strong signals. Unfortunately, most businesses, including real estate, are geared for polishing and maintenance rather than innovation; they change only when the pain of *not* changing becomes severe, when the risk of doing nothing outweighs the risk of doing something different.

Change, especially in today's environment, will happen whether or not we choose to participate. Only those who participate will stay in business, and only those willing and able to innovate will gain the competitive edge. To learn the skill of innovation requires, first and foremost, a vision of your business purpose with all the ambiguity stripped out. Your vision must be stated in language that is clear, specific, detailed, comprehensive, stated in the future perfect tense ("this is how we will have achieved"), stated proactively and compelling enough to elicit the commitment of both yourself and anyone else involved in the business.

*S*tepping Ahead to Profit$

Find a quiet place, close your eyes and move into a future in which your vision has been made real. Imagine you are now a newspaper reporter writing a story on the realization of your vision. As you have achieved what you set out to achieve, what are you seeing, hearing and feeling? Where are you now? How did you get here? What are you doing? Who are the people around you? Now that this vision is complete, do you sense the possibility of a new vision emerging? Write out your story and share it with the one or two people closest to you. Save your story, reread it annually and then repeat this assignment with your new vision. (Adapted from *Strategy of the Dolphin: Scoring a Win in a Chaotic World*, by Dudley Lynch and Paul L. Kordis)

Given a commitment to excellence based on continuous improvement and a clear vision of your business purpose, you will find innovation a natural outcome. Your creative powers will be released because you're open to the future and enthusiastically looking, both consciously and subconsciously, for ideas that will further your vision. Valuable coincidences and synergistic events will surprise you and prove valuable.

Although this may sound more like *Omar Reads the Stars* than a serious business book, it's not. The ability to innovate does require leadership and thinking outside the "MBA box" that structures, and often stagnates, so much of both our planning and operations. Warren Bennis, psychologist, sociologist, economist, professor and former university president, has spent years intensely studying 150 leaders, mostly corporate CEOs. The indispensable first quality of true leaders is, according to Bennis, "a guiding vision ... a strongly defined sense of purpose. Leaders," he continues, "are people who do the right things. Managers are people who do things right. There's a profound difference. When you think about doing the right things, your mind immediately goes toward thinking about the future, thinking about dreams, missions, visions, strategic intent, purpose. But when you think about doing things right, you think about control mechanisms. You think about how-to." Working in an environment created by a leader releases the innovative power of both agents and staff, resulting in ideas that build the competitive edge.

If innovation still seems a bit esoteric, perhaps some examples will make it more concrete.

Niche marketing. Although this idea is old, implementation is always innovative. The goal is to be everything to one select group of people (e.g., retirees, small investors, divorcing spouses, FSBOs, a relatively small geographic area) rather than spreading your efforts thin by trying to appeal to everyone. As reported in the September 1993 issue of *Florida* REALTOR®, John

Surge, of Hobbs/Henderson Advertising in Santa Ana, California, has been developing specialized marketing programs for real estate professionals. There are, according to Surge, four steps to defining your niche:

1. Review local advertising/promotional materials to determine which niches might have room for one more or are not being serviced.
2. Review fair-housing laws, as excluding certain types of clients may be against the law.
3. Analyze your sales for the past year, as you may already be appealing to certain types of buyers or sellers.
4. Anticipate trends, as you may find a niche that no one has discovered yet.

Once an appropriate niche has been determined, the next step is to communicate your niche specialty to the potential consumers of your services.

An excellent example of such niche marketing is Kit Riley's Sage Blossom Consulting (303-440-4227). A longtime residential generalist in Boulder, Colorado, Kit had the opportunity several years ago to market a bed-and-breakfast property. Because she liked the business, she became involved in other bed-and-breakfasts and has now become a recognized expert in this very popular niche. Her education has also expanded: Because she needed knowledge about the qualities of a good investment, she took the CCIM courses and in 1995 obtained her designation, having sold enough bed-and-breakfasts to qualify.

Agent benefits package. Most firms provide services to their agents, as broker-owners recognize that the agents are their customers. Weber Realty Group of metropolitan New Orleans, however, has developed an extensive and well-packaged list of benefits that the company says (as reported in the September 1993 issue of *REAL Trends*) means "more money, more choices and more control" for agents. These benefits include, but certainly are not limited to, a pyramid-style profit-sharing plan available to associates who help the company recruit new agents, flexible and varied commission options, educational funding, discounted health benefits, a compensated mentor program and an agent advisory board of directors. Perhaps the most innovative part of this program is the effective way in which Weber merchandises these benefits to both its associates and other agents.

---

*S*tepping Ahead to Profit$

To trigger your thinking outside the box, your innovative skill, answer this question: "What do I believe is impossible but, if it could be done, would fundamentally change my business for the better?" Record your answer in brief, bulleted statements. Prioritize these statements from the most to the least rewarding. Next, focus on the statement that would result in the greatest benefit and make a list of all the things that could help you achieve the idea embodied in that statement. Prioritize these from the most to the least effective in helping you to achieve your goal. Develop an implementation plan that incorporates these ideas. When you've achieved this first goal, return to the other statements and repeat the process with the next most rewarding.

St. Francis of Assisi succinctly described the reality of this approach when he said, "Start by doing what's necessary; then do what's possible; and suddenly you are doing the impossible."

Excellence and innovation, although absolutely necessary for any agent or firm that intends to deal effectively with the rapidly changing future we perceive, are not sufficient in and of themselves. Just as a three-legged stool cannot stand on two legs, the skill of anticipation must be added to excellence and innovation to not only survive but thrive in 21st-century real estate.

Anticipation

The changes currently under way in the real estate industry are comprehensive and complex. It is likely that a large part of the REALTOR® community does not yet realize the need for change or understand how critical *anticipating* and participating in further change is for survival in the marketplace. For the REALTORS® to remain integral to the real estate process, they must quickly recognize the need for change, and immediately begin to take steps to recover and *anticipate* future change. (Excerpted from the 1994 business plan for NAR's Real Estate Information Network/REIN [now called the REALTOR® Information Network/RIN])

A simpler and perhaps more powerful way of stating this need for anticipatory skill comes from hockey great Wayne Gretzky: "It's not where the puck *is* that counts, it's where the puck *will be*." The goal of accurate anticipation, whether in hockey or real estate, is that it provide you with information that allows you to be in the right place at the right time. Being in the right place at the right time is not a matter of luck but of (1) being aware of changes occurring both within the real estate industry and in the social, economic and political world that surrounds us; (2) anticipating and evaluating the effects of these changes; and, finally, (3) managing the most critical effects by restructuring, reorganizing, redesigning and refocusing the way we conduct our business.

The preceding chapters are designed to sensitize you to the quality and quantity of changes described in (1). There are many other books and articles written and consultants available to assist with (3); that is not the purpose of this book. Therefore, we'll turn our attention to (2), the third leg of our stool: anticipation and evaluation.

Without good anticipation, we all have a tendency to react—to move from one crisis to the next, fighting fires and whacking at the alligators. The result is exhaustion of people, resources and money. This will be increasingly true for those businesses that fail to recognize the need for change, that rely on past successes and fail to anticipate the new demands of the marketplace. As we've seen in previous chapters, these demands can be generalized as (1) consumers who are both more knowledgeable and more demanding; (2) a work force that has different values and expectations and, overall, is more independent; and (3) technology that makes the entire world more sophisticated, complex and yet interdependent.

Given the above, we must learn to anticipate, but how? As we've already concluded that change is happening very rapidly at the same time its very nature is changing, it should be quite clear that the future that we hope to anticipate cannot be predicted accurately, in spite of Lewis Carroll's observation that "It's a poor sort of memory that only works backward." There are, however, two techniques that have proven effective in dealing with our mercurial future.

Scanning the Horizon

The simplest is based on the old but true adage, "The present holds the seeds of the future." When we look back into history, we find times that seem very different from today, but we can also see the beginnings of each change and trace it to its present expression. Most changes are evolutionary, happening in small increments that, over time, result in a large change. A few are revolutionary and breakthrough in character. But even these have their precedent underpinnings and are usually the result of similar events happening almost simultaneously in geographically separate areas—for example, the fall of communism in Eastern Europe, the dominance of buyer agency and the disappearance of subagency.

The first technique, then, is to *look for changes* occurring in your marketplace, determine if similar events are occurring in other parts of the country and incorporate these changes into your business—then you'll be ready for whatever comes tomorrow. One of the easiest ways to identify changes as they are happening is to watch for people who appear to be "messing around" with the rules.

---

*S*tepping Ahead to Profit$

Once a month, visit a book or magazine store. Spend two hours browsing through publications in fields other than your own—for example, technology—that may affect your life and your business. Make a list of specific ways in which these new ideas may change your world; then monitor these ideas for the next 6–12 months. For any that seem to be approaching reality, begin implementing plans to incorporate them into your world.

Keeping Your Eye on the Puck

The second technique is *scenario planning.* If we think about Wayne Gretzky's puck and had Gretzky's knowledge and experience, we'd know that, given where the puck is now, there are only a few places it will probably go next. We could therefore anticipate those places, our senses would monitor the puck as it moved and we'd have a series of alternative plans for what to do should the puck go to any of those places.

Scenario planning for a business is basically the same exercise. Its success is largely dependent on the knowledge and experience of those doing the planning. Likewise, it's an exercise that must be monitored constantly as long as you stay in the game. There are four basic steps to scenario planning:

1. Identify those factors on which the future will depend by scanning the possibilities, focusing on those you believe will have the most impact on your future.
2. Establish a (computer-assisted) system for monitoring those factors.
3. Brainstorm scenarios that describe the futures those factors would create and the changes necessary in your business should any of those futures occur (don't forget that one or more futures might result from interaction of one or more factors).
4. Based on the results of your monitoring, identify deviations from the visualized futures and readjust your scenarios.

This is a very powerful and very effective technique that is slowly replacing strategic planning in corporations, the military and associations. It has sufficient complexity to deal with a complex future and absolutely requires both computerized monitoring and experienced consultants. It allows no sacred assumptions and thus grants the strong possibility that the future will *not* be like the past. Perhaps the best book written on the subject is *The Long View*, by Peter Schwartz.

According to Charles Thomas, a senior scientist with The Futures Group, "Scenario planning is inherently a learning process. Human beings are natural learners, and learning brings us satisfaction." However, in spite of valid, satisfying methods for learning to anticipate and therefore manage the future, few of us do it very well. One reason is explained by Peter M. Senge, MIT professor and author of the business bestseller *The Fifth Discipline* (New York: Doubleday, 1990): "Unfortunately, the primary institutions of our society are oriented predominantly toward controlling rather than learning, and for rewarding individuals for performing for others rather than cultivating their natural curiosity and impulse to learn."

Degrees of Foresight

Another, more biologic and therefore basic reason has been discovered by British scientist Elliott Jaques. After more than 30 years of research, Jaques found that people can be organized into seven groups based on how far into the future they can see (their time horizons) themselves committing to—that is, the time period over which they can formulate goals and carry them to completion. This ability to visualize the future ranges from three months for the shortest group to some 50 years for the longest.

Not surprisingly, Jaques further found that a person's work capacity and the job for which he/she is suited varies with this ability to anticipate the future (see Figure 11.3). Russian neurosurgeon A. R. Luria, who studied data from 40,000 pre-frontal lobotomies, in part confirmed Jaques' work. Luria concluded that the frontal lobes of the human brain are involved in a "program which ensures not only that the subject reacts to actual stimuli, but within certain limits foresees the future, foretells the probability that a particular event may happen, will be prepared if it does happen and, as a result, prepares a program of behavior." Given that there is variation in all living things, it makes sense that there would also be variation in the brain's ability to deal with the future.

FIGURE 11.3   Time Horizons/Thought Characteristics

Time Horizon	Thought Characteristics
Out to 3 months or less.	Rule anchored, likes things very concrete, works with only one dimension at a time, seldom questions tasks.
Out to 1 year.	Seeks judgment and action within the rules, accepts some diversity but handles by immediately dividing different things into piles.
Out to 2 years.	Extrapolates from a given rule, starts with rules and works outward.
Out to 5 years.	Searches for, then maintains an underlying rule structure; will deal with considerable "untidiness" but assumes that in the chaos there are rules and underlying themes to be discovered.
Out to 10+ years.	Makes the rules and feels free to ignore them if they don't fit current circumstances, readily generates alternatives, gives importance to what isn't known/hasn't happened/ hasn't been said.

What this means for the business intent on improving its anticipatory skills is that some people are better at foreknowledge, at thinking about the future, than are others. Therefore, when selecting a group to brainstorm and plan for the future, don't be frustrated with those who have narrow time horizons and appear judgmental and rule-oriented. Instead, choose those who show a willingness to tolerate ambiguity. According to Jaques, such people have valuable qualities for the job of anticipation.

They view uncertainty as a resource, think outside the rules, are willing to generate theories, use contradictory information, are open to all sources, pay attention to what's left unsaid and look for more than one answer.

Future Thoughts

To take advantage of Pogo's "insurmountable opportunities" and effectively plan for an unknown future, the individual agent and the firm must develop three primary skills: excellence, innovation and anticipation. Any one or two is insufficient; all three must be present to sustain success in the future. The combination creates a synergy that will truly yield a sustainable competitive edge.

Learning these important skills requires commitment, purpose and following the suggestions in this chapter. There is almost no training; however, there are many fine books and articles that will help and a handful of outstanding consultants. The greatest assistance, however, will come from forming a small group of people with similar desires to learn and practice these critical skills. It's not necessary that the people in the group all be in real estate; in fact, different perspectives may provide great benefit. As you implement techniques like TQM and scenario planning, share your experiences and learn from one another.

The only sure way of discovering the future is to wait until it's upon us, but that will be too late. You will have lost your competitive edge, and success will be difficult if not impossible to retrieve. Tracking the future by being sensitive to the paradigm shifts we've presented and implementing relevant change in your business by using your skills of excellence, innovation and anticipation is not only worthwhile but exciting. **The future of real estate is here, and you *will* profit from the revolution!**

$\mathcal{S}$tepping Ahead to Profit$

Complete the form below by listing across the top two or more significant changes that you believe will occur five years from now. Beneath each, list the key indicators of this change that you would expect to see now and during each of the next four years. Find at least two other people who have also completed this form and compare your predictions with theirs. Review your form at least annually, checking off those indicators that have been actualized, and repeat the assignment with at least two more expected changes.

Changes I think will happen five years from now

1. _____

2. _____

3. _____

4. _____

Key Indicators	Change 1	Change 2	Change 3	Change 4
Now				
One year from now				
Two years from now				
Three years from now				
Four years from now				
Five years from now				

BIBLIOGRAPHY

A Brief Bibliography of Great Guides for Creating the Future

Albrecht, Karl. *The Northbound Train*. AMACOM, 1994. ISBN: 0-8144-0233-X.

Albrecht, Karl. *The Only Thing That Matters*. Harper Business, 1992. ISBN: 0-88730-541-5.

Albrecht, Karl. *Service Within*. DowJones-Irwin, 1990. ISBN: 1-55623-353-1.

Annison, Michael H. *Managing the Whirlwind*. Medical Group Management Association, 1993. ISBN: 1-56829-029-2.

Bardwick, Judith M. *Danger in the Comfort Zone: From Boardroom to Mailroom—How to Break the Entitlement Habit That's Killing American Business*. AMACOM, 1995. ISBN: 0-8144-7886-7.

Barker, Joel. *The Future Edge: Discovering the New Paradigm of Success*. William Morrow & Co., 1992. ISBN: 0-6881-0936-5.

Barker, Joel. *Paradigms: The Business of Discovering the Future*. Harper Business, 1992. ISBN: 0-88730-647-0.

Bridges, William. *Managing Transitions*. Addison-Wesley Publishing Co., 1991. ISBN: 0-201-55073-3.

Byhan, William C., with Jeff Cox. *Zapp! The Lightning of Empowerment: How to Improve Quality, Productivity and Employee Satisfaction.* Fawcett Columbine, 1988. ISBN: 0-449-90705-8.

Carlson, Jan. *Moments of Truth: New Strategies for Today's Customer-Driven Economy.* Harper & Row, 1987. ISBN: 0-06-091580-3.

Champy, James, and Michael Hammer. *Reengineering Management.* Harper Business, 1995. ISBN: 0-88730-698-5.

Chappell, Tom. *The Soul of Business.* Bantam Doubleday, 1993. ISBN: 0-55309-423-8.

Collins, James C., and Porras, Jerry I. *Built to Last: Successful Habits of Visionary Companies.* Harper Business, 1994. ISBN: 0-88730-671-3.

Gleick, James. *Chaos: Making a New Science.* Penguin Books, 1987. ISBN: 0-14-00.9250-1.

Hammer, Michael, and James Champy. *Reengineering the Corporation.* Harper Collins, 1993. ISBN: 0-88730-640-3.

Handy, Charles. *The Age of Paradox.* Harvard Business School Press, 1994. ISBN: 0-87584-643-2.

Kanter, Rosabeth Moss. *When Giants Learn to Dance: The Definitive Guide to Corporate America's Changing Strategies for Success.* Simon & Schuster, 1990. ISBN: 0-671-69625-4.

Kawasaki, Guy. *Selling the Dream: How to Promote Your Product, Company, or Ideas and Make a Difference Using Everyday Evangelism.* Harper Business, 1991. ISBN: 0-88730-600-4.

Kreigel, Robert J., and Louis Patler. *If It Ain't Broken ... Break It!* Warner Books, 1991. ISBN: 0-446-39359-2.

Lynch, Dudley, and Paul L. Kordis. *Strategy of the Dolphin: Scoring a Win in a Chaotic World.* Fawcett Columbine, 1988. ISBN: 0-449-90529-2.

McNally, David. *Even Eagles Need a Push: Learning to Soar in a Changing World.* Bell Publishing Co., 1994. ISBN: 0-440-50611-5.

Mattimore, Bryan W. *99% Inspiration: Tips, Tales & Techniques for Liberating Your Business Creativity.* AMACOM, 1994. ISBN: 0-8144-7788-7.

Michalko, Michael. *Thinkertoys: A Handbook of Business Creativity for the 90s.* Ten Speed Press, 1991. ISBN: 0-89815-408-1.

Nadler, Gerald, and Shozo Hibino. *Breakthrough Thinking.* Primia Publishing, 1990. ISBN: 1-55958-004-6.

Negroponte, Nicholas. *Being Digital.* Alfred A. Knopf, 1995. ISBN: 0-679-43919-6.

Peppers, Don, and Martha Rogers. *The One to One Future.* Doubleday Currency, 1993. ISBN: 0-385-42528-7.

Peters, Tom. *The Tom Peters Seminar: Crazy Times Call for Crazy Organizations.* Vintage Books, 1994. ISBN: 0-679-75493-8.

Pritchett, Price. *New Work Habits for a Radically Changing World.* Dallas, Texas: Prichett & Associates, 1995.

Primozic, Kenneth, Edward Primozic and Joe Leben. *Strategic Choices: Supremacy, Survival, or Sayonara.* McGraw-Hill, Inc., 1991. ISBN: 0-07-051036-9.

Schwartz, Peter. *The Art of the Long View.* Doubleday & Co., 1995. ISBN: 0-385-26731-2.

Senge, Peter M. *The Fifth Discipline.* Doubleday Currency, 1990. ISBN: 0-385-26094-6.

Sewell, Carl, and Paul B. Brown. *Customers for Life: How to Turn That One-Time Buyer into a Lifetime Customer.* Doubleday Currency, 1990. ISBN: 0-385-41503-6.

Tapscott, Don. *The Digital Economy: Promise and Peril in the Age of Networked Intelligence.* McGraw-Hill, Inc., 1995. ISBN: 0-07-062200-0.

Tapscott, Don, and Art Caston. *Paradigm Shift: The New Promise of Information Technology.* McGraw-Hill, Inc., 1993. ISBN: 0-07-062857-2.

Tomasko, Robert M. *Rethinking the Corporation: The Architecture of Change.* AMACOM, 1993. ISBN: 0-8144-50229.

Treacy, Michael, and Fred Wiersma. *The Discipline of Market Leaders: Choose Your Customers.* Addison-Wesley Publishing Co., 1995. ISBN: 0-201-40648-9.

Webster, Frederick E. Jr. "Defining the New Marketing Concept." *Marketing Management,* Winter 1994 (vol. 2, no. 4, pp. 23–31), American Marketing Association.

Wheatley, Margaret. *Leadership and the New Science.* Berrett-Koehler Publishers, 1992. ISBN: 1-881052-01-X.

Zemke, Ron, with Dick Schaaf. *The Service Edge: 101 Companies That Profit from Customer Care.* A Plume Book, 1989. ISBN: 0-452-26493-6.

Index

195